THRIVING THROUGH CANCER

How I Conquered the Medical, Personal and Professional Impacts of Cancer

Dan Engel

Patient True Talk Publishing

SAN DIEGO, CA

Dan Engel/Patient True Talk Publishing
1325 Pacific Highway, Unit 105
San Diego, CA 92101
www.thrivingthrucancer.com

Thriving Through Cancer/ Dan Engel. -- 1st ed.
ISBN
978-1-7320323-0-9 (Paperback)

TABLE OF CONTENTS

CHAPTER ONE

Prologue

It was the top of the first inning and the Angels were down nine to nothing to the Red Sox. Up first was the ever-tenacious Kyle Wyborney, a member of the Angels his entire career. He made his way to the plate slowly, his steely eyes fixed on the pitcher. You could tell he would not be deterred from leading off the inning with a hit. The pitcher wound up and let go a pitch right down the heart of the plate. Kyle's muscles tensed as he swung the bat and connected. As he struck the ball mightily, the announcer roared with approval, "Open the window Aunt Edna, here it comes!"

Kyle appeared to struggle, the crowd unsure if he could make it out of the batter's box. But I knew better. His mother Donna had told me in advance that Kyle had been practicing all week to walk without his walker for the first time in public. You see, this was the Miracle League of San Diego, a baseball league for children with disabilities, and Kyle was a five-year old with multiple disabilities including one leg shorter than the other and an outturned foot that required him to use a walker. His buddy took his walker from him while Kyle struggled to gain his balance. And as he walked slowly to first base, a determined look on his face, the crowd began to realize the miracle they were witnessing. We had watched Kyle for two seasons now and were accustomed to his smile whenever he worked his way onto the field. But his smile was not to be found. Rather, he was gritting his teeth because walking was so difficult for him. Kyle never stopped walking and by the time he rounded third base and headed for home, the entire crowd was on its feet giving him a standing ovation. The Red Sox players were cheering as well. When Kyle reached home, he slid face down onto home plate. I'm not sure whether he intended to slide or fell out of exhaustion, but either way, he had hit a home run to lead off the inning. There wasn't a dry eye in the crowd as we all turned to one another and shared a Miracle League moment. When he rose again, his buddy brought back his walker and helped him make his way to the dugout. When the second and final inning came around, and Kyle was now the final batter with his team trailing by a run, we witnessed the same miracle again. Kyle walked all the way home, slid onto the plate and tied the score to end the game.

This miracle would not have been possible but for my own miracle. I am a stage four melanoma survivor and at the time of my peak battles with this killer disease, there were no cures and few options. When my diagnosis went from stage three to stage four in 2005, I was told that my chances of living five years were less than five percent. But I made it past those five years and then some. I've been through ten surgeries, radiation therapy, gamma knife surgery on a brain tumor, six clinical trials (chemotherapy, immunotherapy, vaccine, combinations) and seven years of a maintenance clinical trial. My last clinical trial was pivotal in the FDA approving the immunotherapy drug Yervoy as a front-line treatment for metastatic melanoma.

Yervoy was the first drug approved for melanoma in more than 15 years and the first one proven to prolong life.

During about two years of virtually non-stop treatments and surgeries, creating the Miracle League of San Diego was the mission that drove me and kept me from thinking about myself and my condition. Between various treatments, I would attend community meetings, lead board and volunteer meetings, fund-raise or work with our partners on design issues. I remember speaking in front of a planning commission in the midst of bi-ochemotherapy when my body was ravaged by five highly toxic chemicals and my strength was minimal. We didn't get what we wanted that evening, but I persevered and kept fighting. During this journey, I learned a great many things about myself and my capacity for making a difference in the lives of others. I hope this book can inspire you to find your passion as well. I'm living proof that it's never too late and you're never too old to make positive changes in your life.

I also wrote this book because I was fortunate throughout my 15-year journey to have learned much about the process that can help anybody going through similar health issues, whether cancer or some other chronic disease. I have experienced the intersecting circles of the medical, personal and professional lives that can serve as a roadmap to patients and caregivers. For those of you who don't want to get bogged down in the details, I have included *Lessons Learned* at the end of most chapters.

I have learned that some of the people you most expect to be helpful and empathetic are the least adept at dealing with your situation. Conversely, I've learned that some of the people you least expect to be helpful and empathetic get it the most and become rocks for you. My stories are just my stories – things I've experienced along the way. Many of you will face challenges similar to mine, feel my feelings and encounter the same types of people. I hope my stories help you realize you are not alone in experiencing what you're experiencing.

Let me start by saying I'm not a fan of those celebrities like Lance Armstrong who've said that cancer was the best thing to ever happen to them (although he has used his celebrity to profoundly impact many cancer patients and their families). Melissa Etheridge said, "I always tell people I'm grateful for my cancer diagnosis because it was the greatest gift because it completely changed my life." I don't believe that cancer is a gift nor that anyone really is grateful they got cancer. However, I firmly believe that cancer is a wake-up call, an opportunity to discover or rediscover what is important to you in life. I am fortunate that I heeded this wake-up call and discovered that I had a higher calling in life than the career path I had been pursuing for over 20 years. Nonetheless, had I not taken my career path, I might never have had the financial opportunity to engage in these more selfless endeavors.

I'm also writing this book to share my profound gratitude to the doctors and nurses who've cared for me over the years and saved my life. While the doctors direct the decisions, make the incisions, prescribe medicines, etc., it is the nurses who are on the front lines and provide the first and most important connection. Sandy Binder, Cathy Webb, Secela Evans, Mary Beth Watson, Blanca Ledezma, Rebecca Rosenthal, Helen Blohm, Jolie Snively, Angelina Ortiz, you are the best second family I could ever have. Your love and compassion are limitless, and I couldn't have survived as I did without you. It never ceases to amaze me how much you give to all of your patients and still manage to be happy. You face so much pain and sorrow, and too few of the miracles like me. You have my ultimate gratitude, love and respect. Maria Estrada, thank you for always greeting me with a smile and making sure I got to the right place at the right time. In order of treatment, Rick Essner, Bob Wollman, Jeff Weber, Steve O'Day, Peter Boasberg and Omid Hamid, you guys are the best doctors on the planet. Keith Flaherty, Jedd Wolchock, Ruth Halaban, it's so gratifying to have you in my corner as well. Collectively you represent the best options available to a melanoma patient in the United States. I will continue to refer patients to you based on geography.

So many friends to thank, but a few stand out for their direct impact on my well-being. Your love and devotion to me is unparalleled. Andy Astrachan who is an amazing friend, colleague, boss, mentor and advocate. Sid Ferenc who is likewise an amazing friend, colleague, boss, mentor and advocate. Judy Petraitis for always being there for me and giving me a bed for my overnight visits to Los Angeles. Ilan Bialer, I could always count on you, and though it came out the wrong end, thanks for bringing that Langer's Pastrami Sandwich before I started biochemotherapy. Jamie Johnson, you accompanied me to USC at one of my more worrisome appointments and visited often. My cousin Jeff Katz, you've been with me through so much of life experiences and were there whenever I needed you. Dave Altman, Scott Krishel and Alton Kuperman, you were my rocks in San Diego. Chris McGovern and Scott Schumann, you were my East Coast rocks. I need to recognize my family who were there for me whenever called upon – my parents Sandy and Morrie, my brothers David and Jon, my sister Deborah, and their spouses and children.

To my children Sam and Jordan, you are the reason I fought so hard to stay alive. I couldn't imagine not being there for you at each milestone in your life. I couldn't imagine not being there for you during any adversity. I couldn't imagine not being with you and loving you. Each milestone I made, we moved the goal to the next one. I am so proud of how you've grown into these wonderful young adults who are smart, caring, compassionate, interesting, giving and aware. I love you more than you can imagine and more than I can demonstrate. I hope my sharing this story makes you proud as well. Keep being who you are and keep learning. If there's one lesson from my career path that I can share with you it's that whenever I stopped learning in a job it was time for a change. I am truly grateful to your mother Suzie for helping to raise you right and mold you into who you are today.

Finally, some thanks to my dear Robin. You brought love back in to my life when I needed it most. Your warmth, love, belief in me, compassion and support has changed me for the better. You've brought a smile back to my face and given me another person and family to love. I wake up thrilled to be next to you and go to bed thankful that you are in my life. Your free and flexible spirit is the perfect offset to my rigidity. Your passion for life, family and friends fuels my passion for the same. I love you with all my soul.

CHAPTER TWO

Background

This is a story about melanoma, the deadliest form of skin cancer. It is a story about how against very long odds I am still alive and thriving to tell this story. So, in the words so memorably sung by Julie Andrews in *The Sound of Music,* "let's start at the very beginning, a very good place to start."

I grew up in Los Angeles in the 1960s with two older brothers and a younger sister. I had two older brothers David and Jon, and a younger sister Deborah. My father Morris was a CPA who worked very long hours while my mother Sandy was a stay-at-home mom who cooked dinners every night, attended all of our sporting events and basically ran the household.

On the first day of every summer our family went to Santa Monica Beach and we dutifully walked across the long sand with our beach chairs and my dad's army blanket that served as our beach blanket. We had the express purpose of getting the first burn that over the course of the summer would turn into the perfect tan. We never wore hats and never wore sunscreen. I'm not sure we even knew that there was a product called sunscreen. Rather, in between spending hours in the waves body surfing and exposing our heads and bodies to the most dangerous rays of the sun, we would lay on the beach slathered in sun tan products like Coppertone, that promised a golden tan, or Bain de Soleil, for that Saint Tropez tan. Those of you from that generation will undoubtedly remember the Bain de Soleil jingle. Some even used Johnson's Baby Oil instead.

We always spent the last ten days of summer either at a beachfront hotel in San Diego or later in Laguna Beach. We vacationed with several other families and spent all day on the beach, in the ocean or in the pool. My father played two card games with the other fathers, hearts or gin, and as I got older I joined in. We would spend hours playing in the sun and only took breaks when it got too hot and we needed a dip in the ocean to cool off. Again, we never had sunscreen and I never wore a hat.

When we weren't at the beach, we were hanging out at the elementary school playground playing softball, basketball, and other games, or just running around. We went on field trips to the zoo or Catalina Island or Los Angeles Dodgers baseball games. And we never covered up. Never. In fact, more often than not we would be shirtless when we could, further exposing ourselves to the sun. Little did we know that the cumulative effects of sun damage from our youth could turn into deadly skin cancer as we got older.

Winters were mild as well and being outside was just what we did. After school, we would play football or throw baseballs in the streets. There was ample recess time in the 1960s and recess was always outdoors, unless it rained, which it didn't often. High school was no different other than we had more freedom to go to the beach in the summer.

I was an undergraduate student at UCLA where I continued my sun worshipping days, although I don't think many people would have described me that way. It was more a function of the fact that I would sit in the same outdoor dining area every day for an hour or two, usually in the peak sun hours. Again, I never wore a hat and never put on sunscreen. If we had the time and the day was exceptionally nice, we would put a towel down on one of UCLA's large lawn areas, take off our shirts, and soak up the rays in between classes.

After four years at UCLA, I went to UC Berkeley for a four-year combined JD/MBA program (law and business). While the sun wasn't as strong in Northern California as it was in Southern California, the same rules applied. Sit in the sun as much as possible, closing my eyes for nap time whenever I could. I started to play golf and intramural softball, which gave me more opportunities to be in the sun. It's not that I played sports every day, it's more that when I did participate in outdoor sports, I was exposed to the sun for hours at a time without any protection.

I moved to New York directly after graduate school to work on Wall Street. When you were a young investment banker, summer weekends (when you weren't in the office) were spent in the Hamptons, which consisted of several towns on the east end of Long Island. My best friends and I shared a house in the town of Amagansett. Weekends were spent as follows. We took the Long Island Railroad from Grand Central Station to Amagansett on Friday night. We woke up Saturday morning and walked to the farmer's market to buy produce and incredible baked goods. After a quick breakfast, we walked to the beach with our beach chairs, towels, and a week's worth of mandatory reading material. We would spend four to six hours on the beach, alternating between the ocean, reading and napping. We would then walk to the fish market to buy dinner to BBQ on our grill. Sunday morning was an exact replay of Saturday except we spent less time at the beach to make the 3:30 train back to New York City. Did we ever put on sunscreen? Not a chance. The first weekend was always dedicated to that first burn that would ultimately lead to the perfect tan. We told ourselves that we looked healthy when we were tan. Years later science told us differently.

I met my wife Suzie my last summer in New York. We got married in April 1991 in San Diego and went to Hawaii for our honeymoon. Suzie and I moved to Manhattan Beach, a quaint beach city about 20 miles south of my parents' home shortly after we were married. Although we were often in the sun in Manhattan Beach, playing tennis or golf, by this point we understood the importance of sunscreen. Our son Sam was born in 1994 and our daughter Jordan in 1997.

I continued to work in the investment banking industry and Suzie worked at the tennis club at which we belonged. I was now working at a very small firm for a guy named Andy Astrachan who would become a very important mentor in my life. Andy ran a boutique investment banking firm where he gave me all the responsibility I could handle and all the opportunity to succeed. He was kind, compassionate, intelligent, warm, giving, caring and fair.

This is a good place to acknowledge something that is probably obvious. I was fortunate to grow up fairly privileged and well-off. These circumstances provided me access to education, doctors and other things throughout my journey that might not be as readily accessible to the vast majority of readers. I am certain this privilege had a meaningful impact on my outcome, though it shouldn't.

CHAPTER THREE

The Initial Diagnosis

I can vividly recall everything about my original cancer diagnosis in November 1998. I had just gotten a very short haircut and was sitting on the steps in my Manhattan Beach house playing with my one-and-a-half-year-old daughter Jordan. We happened to have a large skylight bisecting our house directly above the staircase and it was a sunny day. My wife walked over and noticed a spot on my scalp. She suggested I see a dermatologist, which I had never done in my life (I was 36 at the time). I got a referral to a dermatologist and made an appointment. The dermatologist took a biopsy and I was to await the results. Two days later I received a call from the dermatologist (not an assistant – the first clue that it is bad news) who said he would like to see me to discuss the results. I asked him when he wanted to see me, and he replied, another huge red flag, "you tell me, I'll fit you in." I was a self-important investment banker who had a conference call in a half hour, so I said I would come in after the call. All the time I was driving I was having conversations in my head about what the dermatologist could possibly say. I don't really know what I was thinking when I put the work call first but by the time I arrived at my office I realized that no conference call was that important and asked a colleague to cover the call for me. I called my wife to tell her what was going on and I went straight to the doctor's office.

The doctor proceeded to explain that the biopsy indicated I had stage two melanoma based on a Clark's Level 2 with a 15% chance that it had spread in my body.[1] The dermatologist further explained that a surgeon would need to excise the tumor with a margin of about an inch in all directions. The tumor itself looked like a scab about the size of a fingernail. Based on the full diameter of over two inches, I would need a skin graft to close the incision since skin on the scalp could not stretch that far. He then sent me to the John Wayne Cancer Institute ("JWCI") in Santa Monica, one of the leading melanoma centers in the world. Not only was the JWCI a top melanoma center but it trained more surgical oncologists than almost any other center in America. A surgical oncologist differs from a general surgeon in that s/he has completed a surgical oncology fellowship program approved by the Society of Surgical Oncology and focuses on the surgical management of tumors, especially cancerous tumors. This was my first example of being fortunate to live in a city and be a patient of well-informed doctors who could send me to world-class specialists. Without a doubt this good fortune is a primary reason I am alive today.

I called my wife and she found a neighbor to watch our two children and she met me at the surgeon's office. Dr. Richard Essner confirmed everything the dermatologist said and discussed the surgery and recovery in more detail. He also

---

[1] In 1998, initial staging for melanoma was based on the Clark's Level of invasion, or the number of layers of skin penetrated by the tumor. In 2010 the American Joint Commission on Cancer ("AJCC") updated its staging criteria based on newer information and the Clark's Level became less important. Moreover, the AJCC added sublevels to each stage.

explained that they would employ a technique developed at the JWCI to find the sentinel node and determine whether the cancer had spread to any lymph nodes. Prior to surgery, a technician would inject blue dye directly into the tumor and I would lay still for two hours while the die would progress through my lymphatic system to what is known as the sentinel node. During surgery, Dr. Essner would find the sentinel node and remove only this lymph node through a much less invasive procedure than prior standard of care wherein the surgeon would remove all lymph nodes from the lymph basin where the cancer would have likely spread. The pathology lab would then biopsy this lymph node and if there was no evidence of disease, it would be deemed that the cancer had not spread, and I would be spared a full lymph dissection. This "sentinel node technique" became the gold standard in melanoma care as well as other cancers.

We had a family vacation to Hawaii for Thanksgiving in a few days and I had a choice to make – cancel the trip and have the surgery immediately or wait until we returned. The decision was mine to make as Dr. Essner didn't believe that a two-week delay would have any impact on the cancer. Based upon the low probability that the cancer had spread, I chose to go to Hawaii, whereas my wife, who was much more pessimistic (in fact, we were polar opposites in that respect), would have cancelled the trip.

I took full advantage of the time in Hawaii to relax with family and connect on a very personal level. Scott Krishel, a friend of mine to whom I am deeply indebted, gave me a book to read, *Prepare for Surgery – Heal Faster,* by Peggy Huddleston that helped me immeasurably. I recommend this book to anyone facing a major surgery for the first time as there are many useful tips. The book provides meditation techniques to help reduce anxiety before surgery, use less pain medication and heal faster.

One hallmark of her book is the explanation of how healing statements, words repeated often during surgery, could reduce the use of pain medication by 23-60%. Depending on the statements spoken, they could hasten other recovery challenges such as eating and peeing. I provided my statements to Dr. Essner and my anesthesiologist and instructed them to repeat these words often during the surgery.

Finally, Ms. Huddleston provides instruction on visualization techniques to turn your worries about surgery into positive healing imagery. I learned how to visualize my tumor shrinking and disappearing. She even provided a guided meditation tape that I listened to at least four times a day, almost entirely while resting in a hammock by the water. This proved quite prescient for me.

When we returned a week later, I went in for surgery first thing in the morning. I couldn't believe how relaxed I was able to be as I listened to the guided medication tape while waiting in pre-op. I am so grateful to Scott for giving me this book as it enabled me to eliminate all tension as I went into surgery. I even practiced my guided meditation while needing to remain perfectly still for two hours waiting for the blue dye to trace to my sentinel nodes. I not only visualized myself in my hammock, but I felt myself swaying with the breeze even though I was lying on a cold table.

The surgery lasted about six hours and went well. The reason it took so long, aside from the fact that Dr. Essner is extremely precise and thorough, is that it included four separate incisions. The first was taking the skin graft from my chest. The second was the wide excision on the scalp and placing the skin graft to close the wound. The third was removing tissue from behind the ear that lit up with the blue dye, and the fourth was removing two sentinel nodes that also lit up blue.

I went home the next day. I needed very little pain medication, was able to pee freely and ate solid food (thank you healing statements). As this story continues, you will learn that I always left the hospital as quickly as I could and believe this was very important to overall health.

LESSONS LEARNED

> * ***If possible, be the first surgery patient scheduled for the day***
> * ***There is no magical formula about who and what to tell people about your diagnosis***

One of my first takeaways is to insist, if possible, on being the first patient in the operating room for your surgeon. My surgery lasted six hours and I knew that Dr. Essner scheduled other surgeries after mine. Unfortunately, the scheduling departments for hospitals ask you to check-in at least two hours prior to your "scheduled" surgery. Hence, if the surgeon runs late on the first patient, you can be waiting much longer in the pre-op area where your anxiety increases exponentially as time elapses. Imagine this sequence if you are the third or fourth surgery of the day.

Another decision point is whom to tell about your diagnosis and when. Do you tell extended family? Do you tell friends? Work associates or superiors or both? Faith leaders? These are all personal decisions and it helps to have at least one advocate with you on your journey to help make these decisions. And this decision can and will change over time, especially if you wind up on a long journey like I did. Ultimately, no matter whom you tell, you can't know in advance how they will react to the news. Some people are just better at dealing with cancer or other health issues than others, and they know what to say and how to help. Sometimes I heard things that made no sense and were not comforting at all. I knew that everyone meant well, but I was still surprised at the words that came out of some people's mouths. I was also surprised by some people whom I'd never expected to step up and become among my most helpful, understanding friends.

CHAPTER FOUR

Surgery Number Two (December 1998)

Bad news came within a week. The biopsy of my sentinel nodes determined that the cancer had spread to my lymph nodes and I needed to schedule another surgery ten days after the first to remove all lymph nodes from my neck. It turns out that the original biopsy was not "deep" enough and did not stage me properly. I had stage three melanoma that carried a 50% chance of recurrence. In hindsight, armed with that knowledge, would I have taken the trip to Hawaii? I can't answer that, although I know that the trip was crucial to my mental well-being.

This time the surgery was to remove all of the lymph nodes from the right side of my neck. Again, I checked in early in the morning for an 8:00 a.m. start time. Armed with my headphones and guided meditation tape I was relaxed and ready to go. Dr. Essner cut over the same incision he had used the first time to avoid having a new scar. I appreciated how he thought of the aesthetics in addition to the medical needs.

Post-surgery I would have a Jackson Pratt ("JP") drain hanging from my neck that collected fluids for several days until it was no longer needed. The JP drain consisted of a tube inserted into the bottom of the incision connected to a soft, round squeeze bulb. The quirky thing about a JP drain in the neck is I had to wear a shirt with a chest pocket to "hold" the squeeze bulb so it wasn't just dangling and pulling at the wound and stitches. This was especially important when trying to sleep comfortably. Another crazy thing about have a JP drain is that even though I felt healthy enough to go out in public, the JP drain made me very self-conscious and in addition, made me realize what others might think when they saw me with one. Ultimately, I stayed in or, if I went out, wore something over so others couldn't see the JP drain. I was lucky I only needed the JP drain for a few days.

I had to wait another several days for the pathology results on the lymph nodes that were removed from my neck. Anxiety and stress were particularly high during this time as the results could have a drastic impact on my long-term prognosis. I was fortunate that the pathology reports indicated that no other lymph nodes showed evidence of cancer.

At this point I can say that this experience was my first spiritual awakening. Although not a religiously observant person, I believe that it was God looking down on me and my family when I was sitting under the skylight. That, or I was just lucky to have that short haircut and be sitting under the skylight when my wife walked by. Had we not found the lesion then, it is entirely possible that the cancer would have spread further and killed me before we ever found it.

LESSONS LEARNED

> • *If applicable, use your case as a teaching lesson for others*

An important lesson for me was that my "case" could be a teaching lesson to others who were not aware of what a melanoma lesion might look like nor the consequences of having melanoma. The first time I went back to my hairdresser was eye-opening for me. When she saw my head with about a two-inch diameter chunk of hair missing she almost dropped to the floor. I don't know whether this was from the shock of seeing my head or the realization that months prior she had told me I had a scab on my scalp but never followed up on later appointments and told me that the scab was still there. I calmly explained to her that from now on, if she ever saw a client with a similar scab, she could and should tell my story.

CHAPTER FIVE

My First Clinical Trial

My next step was to determine whether there were any clinical trials to prevent the cancer from recurring (remember I now had a 50% chance of recurrence within five years). As a young, healthy individual, I wanted to try everything in my power to prevent a recurrence. Since there was no proven method for preventing recurrence, it was imperative to me to find at least one clinical trial that might help.

The first thing a patient needs to know when exploring clinical trials is how to properly describe their current diagnosis or state of disease. In my case, I had completely resected melanoma (the term means that I had surgery to remove the cancer and there was no further evidence of disease). Most clinical trials are designed around drugs for treating cancer, not preventing recurrences. Hence my options were extremely limited.

This was another example of how I was fortunate to be treated at the JWCI, as it was at the forefront of melanoma research. I was told by Dr. Essner that there was one clinical trial available at Memorial Sloan Kettering Cancer Center in New York ("MSKCC") and another at the JWCI. The MSKCC trial had two "arms:" one with interferon, the only then-available treatment for melanoma, the other with a placebo. Hence, if I chose to travel to New York City there was a 50% chance I would receive a highly toxic drug that had a moderate effect on treating melanoma and a 50% chance I would receive a placebo.

The JWCI trial, on the other hand, was for an experimental vaccine developed at the JWCI. The vaccine was known as "CancerVax" and was comprised of several known lines of melanoma. This trial also had two arms with a placebo, with one major difference: each arm also was given the drug BCG, which was thought to be helpful in preventing melanoma. To summarize, I had a 50% chance of receiving a totally experimental vaccine plus BCG, or receiving a placebo plus BCG.

My decision was relatively straight forward for three reasons. First, I did not want to fly to New York City multiple times based on a 50% chance of receiving a toxic drug with limited proven benefits. Second, at the JWCI I would at least receive BCG, which had a possibility of providing benefit. Third, and really the clinching fact for me, was that Dr. Essner was able to share with me recently published data that showed that interferon had moved from what was characterized as "statistically significant" benefits on the average to "statistically insignificant" benefits compared to a placebo.

When I shared this decision with my boss at the time, Andy Astrachan, he went out of his way to help. He didn't want me to only have 50% chance of receiving the CancerVax, he wanted me to get it for sure. Amazingly, he called his friend Michael Milken, the former head of Drexel Burnham Lambert, who had himself become involved in supporting medical research surrounding prostate cancer, the cancer that he battled.

In what was one of the more stunning gestures I've experienced, Mr. Milken placed a call to the JWCI asking if they would put me on the CancerVax arm or just give me the drug outright. It was kind of outrageous that he thought he could convince a noted cancer center to ignore all rules and protocols established to ensure unbiased clinical trials and place me where he wanted. What is even more stunning is he didn't know me personally. Such is the power of advocates like Andy who would do anything for you when asked. The JWCI rejected Mr. Milken's request, of course. I expected that decision and applauded it, despite it not being in my best interest. But the clinical trial process, which is so critical to developing new cancer drugs and drugs for other diseases, requires unbiased objective studies, and who was I to expect any special treatment? I am thankful that Andy and Mr. Milken made the effort but embarrassed as well for having participated (albeit inactively) in a blatant attempt to skirt the rules.

The "protocol" for CancerVax required me to get injections every two weeks for the first three months, every month for the next nine months, every two months for the next year, then every three months for three more years. These injections were "subcutaneous," meaning very small needles injected just under the skin surface, and were given in four spots with concentrated lymph node basins: underneath both armpits and in both sides of the groin. The first two injections included the BCG which left distinct marks still visible today. In addition to the four injections, I received one smaller injection on the wrist from which nurses would take two measurements a week later. The measurements were for "edema," or swelling, and "erythema," or redness.

Because the study was "double blind," neither the nurse providing the injection, nor the doctor, nor I, would know whether I was receiving CancerVax or the placebo. The syringes were filled by one nurse I never saw and were wrapped in brown paper, so we could not see the color of the fluid (the placebo would be clear while the CancerVax would have another color). The reason for covering the syringe is that if a patient knew he was receiving the placebo, it is highly likely he would choose to stop his participation in the trial. If patients did that, there would be no reliable way to determine whether those receiving the treatment were being benefited versus those receiving the placebo.

From the very first dose I saw obvious reactions on my skin with a large area of swelling and redness. I guessed that I was receiving CancerVax because in my mind, there was no way my skin would react that way if I was receiving a placebo. I don't know whether this guess was correct, but it seemed that way to me and I had all the incentive in the world to continue on the trial protocol.

Another part of the protocol was the follow up brain MRI and CT scans. These were conducted every six months for the first two years and once a year thereafter. All of my scans were what I called "clean," or showed no evidence of disease (doctors shorten this to "NED") throughout the five years of the trial. In my mind at the end of the five-year trial period, which was the time during which I had a 50% chance of recurrence, I was cancer free.

LESSONS LEARNED

> - *If possible, get treated at a center of excellence for your particular diagnosis*
> - *Treat all caregivers with respect and they in turn will respect and help you*
> - *Nurses are your best friend – treat them as such*

I learned how lucky I was to be treated at a true center of excellence with melanoma experts. Imagine had I been treated at a typical community oncologist's office. It is entirely possible that the oncologist there would not have enough experience with melanoma patients to either recommend a clinical trial or be able to counsel me on the relative merits of each protocol. I also had the benefit of a surgical oncologist who directed me to the research about the available trials. As time went on, I learned about the other resources available online, such as www.clinicaltrials.gov or some of the melanoma support groups. However, those sites are extremely difficult to navigate if you are not a doctor and are not given proper direction by your oncologist.

I learned quite a few other valuable lessons over the course of those five-plus years that have benefited me tremendously. Let's start with how to communicate with and treat people. There is no doubt that one of the most stressful experiences you will ever encounter is when you first learn you have cancer and begin to deal with the consequences and treatments. And very often the people we need to speak to most are protected by gatekeepers who manage their schedules. There is nothing more frustrating than wondering when you will receive your scan, when can you see the doctor, when can you schedule surgery, when do you need to be here, especially when the person on the other end is a non-responsive person. I have encountered so many of those on the other end and the best advice I can give is to be patient with them and to treat them with respect. Rob McLaughlin, who is the front desk person at the JWCI (I met Rob in 1999 and he is still manning that desk), is one of the kindest individuals around. Rob knows every patient and every doctor and does his best to handle your needs based on priorities that only he can understand. For example, you might be worried about the time for surgery a week out and he is trying to schedule a patient who needs surgery within hours. It is so easy to become impatient and mistreat people like Rob when they are doing the best they can. But if you recognize that they are human and treat them with respect and understanding, you are most likely to get quick, constructive feedback on your needs. Call them by their names when they pick up the phone and ask them how they are doing. Take the time to get to know them and they will do the same with you. Believe me, they see so much that can bring them down that having a polite person on the other end of the phone or across the desk from them who cares about them will make their day better. And when their day is better, your response time is quicker, and your information is more accurate.

The same communication advice goes for your nurses. Sandy Binder was the first nurse I met at the JWCI and she would become a key person in my care over the years. I remember getting to know her and her family and remember how sad I was when she moved to Australia. I was really happy when she moved back several years later. You can't understand how important continuity in care is until you reap the benefit or experience the opposite. I developed close relationships with all the nurses I saw on a regular basis and cherish those experiences. Over the years we became family. I got to know my nurses so well that we began to have bets about when Dr. Essner would arrive for my appointments. I knew that Dr. Essner ran perpetually late (because he begins his day by seeing patients in the hospital and he takes his time) and so I made sure to book my appointments for the first one in the day. They may have been 8:00 am or 8:30 am or 9:00 am, but regardless, he was usually not there on time. For fun, I tried to make light of the situation and created bets with the nurses. They appreciated that I could laugh about this, while most patients would fly off the handle when their doctors showed up late. But tardiness is just part of the process when you are seeing oncologists and surgical oncologists who often face emergencies that throw off their schedules. I learned to control what I could, which is how I reacted to chronic lateness, while I could not control any of those external pressures that impacted my doctors' timing. I learned to bring relaxing music on my iPod (and later iPhone) and did my best to stay calm while inevitably waiting.

CHAPTER SIX

What Next?

I'd now had surgery and begun a clinical trial. My next question was whether I could do anything else to prevent a recurrence. I decided the first step was to meet with a nutritionist and determine whether diet could have an impact. There was certainly plenty of anecdotal evidence from individuals that diet "cured" their cancer. Michael Milken claimed that switching to a largely vegetarian diet was a significant factor in his miraculous recovery from prostate cancer. Thankfully there was a nutritionist affiliated with the JWCI.

I found my meeting with the nutritionist extremely informative and helpful. She shared that there was no scientific evidence that diet impacted skin cancer, or melanoma in particular. Rather, she advised me to choose a diet that would generally boost my immune system, as a strong immune system is important in fighting any disease. She recommended a diet low in fat and high in fiber. She gave me reasonable targets of fat grams per day and fiber grams per day and provided a listing of foods that could provide that. Most significantly though, she said the targets could average out over a week, so that some days could be better than others as long as I hit the overall objectives.

Aside from the actual targets chosen for me, none of this information was particularly new to me. The literature was chock full of suggestions that a low fat, high fiber, high in fruits and vegetables diet was the easiest way to boost your immune system. I did learn that it was important to mix up the pigments in vegetables (reds, greens, yellow, oranges) because they contained different nutrients.

The most important lesson the nutritionist gave me, however, was not to think of this as a "diet," but rather as a "lifestyle change." Adopting those words alone changed my mindset about slipping. The typical response when one is on a diet and breaks it for a day or two is to throw up their hands in surrender and just quit the diet because it's too hard. But by viewing these eating habits as a lifestyle change, and setting weekly targets rather than daily limits, I was able to shrug off days when I didn't eat as well as I should because the rest of the time I did eat well. I'm not one to say there is only one diet that works for everyone because I'm not an expert on the subject. But, if you face a similar situation and make a change like this, my nutritionist's advice was spot on. And I was able to maintain this lifestyle change for about six years.

Aside from nutrition, the other obvious place to make lifestyle changes to prevent recurrence was in exercise. I had always been fairly active, and until that point played tennis once or twice a week. I decided to try yoga as another way to bring calmness and balance into my life. Unfortunately, I found during my first yoga class that I had another fitness issue. During one of the poses, I discovered that I couldn't raise my right arm off the ground. It just wouldn't budge and seemed frozen in place. I learned the hard way that post-surgery, one often needs to begin physical therapy as quickly as possible to prevent muscles from atrophying. As talented a surgeon as Dr. Essner is, he is a surgical oncologist first and foremost, meaning he is keenly focused on removing all cancer from your body while he is operating. In all of our follow up, we discussed clinical trials and other steps we could take to prevent recurrence. But we never discussed the need for physical therapy. I asked him to write me a prescription for physical therapy and I began the process to rebuild my neck and shoulder muscles that were damaged from the full neck dissection. Yoga ultimately did not fit my schedule.

At this point I made my first discovery about my priorities. I had young children with very loving and giving grandparents living in San Diego. My wife also had aunts and a sister living close to her parents. I was working for a boutique investment banking firm and I knew that the owner, Andy Astrachan, was winding down the business. I had never before considered moving to San Diego as my family was in Los Angeles and I thought San Diego lacked many of the superficial things I thought precious in Los Angeles (like great restaurants). But, I wondered if I ever got a recurrence, what would I want and need for my family? I realized that I wanted my wife and children to have the support of her family if that ever occurred. One day I looked at her and said, "let's move to San Diego." She was stunned at first, but was excited, so we decided to put our house on the market and begin looking in San Diego. We moved during the summer of 1999 and to this day it is one of the best decisions I've ever made.

For the next four years, I continued on the CancerVax trial at the JWCI and drove to Los Angeles every three months for treatments and scans. I identified a local oncologist who had a nurse perform my skin test readings, so I wouldn't have to drive back to Los Angeles just for a two-minute consult. Eventually, I bought my own measuring instrument (a caliper) and had a doctor friend conduct and report the measurements.

As I needed to be in Los Angeles for these quarterly vaccine appointments and doctor visits, I tried to minimize my time away from work and made all my appointments for the first thing on Monday mornings. This is when I developed my own "protocol" to match my clinical trial protocol. I would drive up on Sunday afternoon and go straight to my friend Ilan Bialer's house. We would then drive to West Hollywood to meet Jamie Johnson, a law school classmate. We would eat dinner at one of the restaurants with street seating, so we could watch the always entertaining crowd. Following dinner, we would typically walk to the Sky Bar at the Mondrian Hotel. Sky Bar was situated around the pool at this very hip hotel that had a great view of the city. For the next two hours or so we would just laugh at all of life's foibles, particularly our own, while enjoying the scenery. The scenery in this case wasn't just the view of the city, but rather, a quite unique slice of pretty people dressed to the nines.

This "boy's night out" routine became an important part of my life. I didn't like to come to Los Angeles anymore because these quarterly trips were not by choice and solely for medical treatment. There was nothing about the purpose of the trips that made them pleasant or desirable experiences. But boy's night out with Ilan and Jamie allowed me to be a little bit normal and take the sting out of driving to Los Angeles only to be stung by needles the next day. I had something to look forward to with

Ilan and Jamie – a respite of love and laughter that wasn't easily replicable anywhere else.

LESSONS LEARNED

> • *Study nutrition and make lifestyle changes to boost your immune system*
> • *Ask your surgeon whether physical therapy will help post-surgery and get a prescription to begin as soon as you feel physically able*

I believe nutrition is an important part of overall health, but it is difficult to discern whether any one diet can really help prevent or cure cancer. This is something every patient should explore, but I advise seeking professional advice. Once you choose to make a change, however, remember that it is a lifestyle change and not a diet. This way you can make it stick longer.

I also learned the importance of asking for a physical therapy prescription to begin as soon as possible post-surgery. Physical therapy is a significant component of recovery and should be utilized as needed. In addition, I learned how to adapt to the protocols of a clinical trial and work around travel requirements by finding fun things to do on my visits to Los Angeles. This is a recurring theme of understanding that you must be your own advocate in the health process – more on this later. Lastly, I remembered that having a large, loving and supporting family is crucial to mental and physical health.

CHAPTER SEVEN

The First Recurrence and Surgery Number Three (December 2004/ January 2005)

In late 2002, I began working for Applied Underwriters, a company that I had financed while working for Andy Astrachan and in which he had invested. I reported directly to the CEO, Sid Ferenc, another important mentor in my life. The company was based in San Francisco with back-office operations in Omaha, Nebraska. When Sid offered me the job, he asked that I establish an office that wasn't in my home and that I travel to San Francisco and Omaha on a regular basis. For the first time in my professional career, I was working at an operating company and not for an investment bank where my income was dependent on closing deals. I enjoyed this transition into an operating business and particularly enjoyed working for Sid.

As I was flying almost weekly, I bought a digital music player (before the iPod was invented) and some over-the-ear noise cancelling headphones to make travel more pleasant. Sometime in mid-2004, about six months after the CancerVax trial ended and I had been declared "NED" (No Evidence of Disease, or in lay-man terms, cancer-free), I began to notice that the headphones felt uncomfortable and there was a small bump behind my right ear. I made an appointment with a local dermatologist as I thought this was just some skin related issue. The dermatologist examined me and said there was nothing to be worried about. He didn't examine my medical history to the extent he should have, and I wasn't far enough along in my journey to understand the need to share more and push harder for more in-depth testing.

By the time December came around, the discomfort turned into a noticeable bump behind my ear on the same side of my neck as the original lymphadenectomy. I went to an ear nose and throat specialist who did a more thorough medical history and took a biopsy. Unfortunately, I got another one of those calls to come in to discuss the results as soon as possible. That couldn't be good news, I thought. Again, to the doctor's office we went only to hear that the bump was a small tumor of melanoma. I immediately called Dr. Essner (I learned an early lesson to get my doctor's cell phone number and call with any emergencies) who ordered scans later that afternoon in Los Angeles to determine the full extent of the cancer. My decision to move to San Diego was indeed prescient as we were able to ask Suzie's parents to watch our children while we drove to Los Angeles.

Because we had at least a two-hour drive to Los Angeles and it would take longer to see Dr. Essner, I knew that I would satisfy the requisite four-hours of no drinking or eating before a CT scan. We saw Dr. Essner first and then he sent us to two separate locations for the MRI and CT scans because those were the only locations that could fit me in under such short notice. Having a close relationship with Dr. Essner was critical in getting these scans scheduled the same day. Most patients I've talked to over the years do not have the same experience and often have to wait several days just to see their oncologist and then several more days to get scans scheduled.

The brain MRI was completed first and then off we went to another scanning facility. This facility had an older CT scan machine that made the test take significantly longer than newer machines. I drank three 16-ounce drinks of cranberry juice laced with barium that was required before the scans. Then I was placed on the CT machine bed and the one-and-a-half-hour test began. Unfortunately, the nurse neglected to tell me to use the restroom prior to the test. There I was lying on the table in a flimsy gown and desperately needing to pee in the middle of the exam. What happened next was probably one of the most humiliated I've ever felt during a medical procedure. A nurse came into the room with a plastic bottle and placed my penis inside the bottle so I could pee. I couldn't move because of the test so I then had to call her back in the room to remove my penis from the bottle. Looking back on this experience I can laugh, but it sure didn't seem too funny at the time.

After this test we drove back to Dr. Essner's office who waited patiently for the test results. Lucky for me, Dr. Essner was able to order "stat" readings by the radiologists and we didn't have to wait very long at his office. The tests confirmed that the melanoma had returned. In addition to the two tumors behind my ear, I had cancer in the parotid gland and some additional lymph nodes in my neck. I would require a five-hour surgery to would remove the two "soft tissue metastases," remove the parotid gland (a "parotidectomy") and remove the lymph nodes from the right side of my neck (my second "lymphadenectomy"). Dr. Essner said the parotidectomy was a tricky surgery as there are five very sensitive nerves around the mouth that could be severed by mistake.

Prior to driving back to San Diego, we started what became a ritual. We went to our favorite sushi restaurant for dinner, Sasabune. The sushi chef, Nobi Kushuhara, was a friend who made every meal I've ever had at Sasabune special. Over time, whenever I needed to chill and think about medical treatments or surgeries or clinical trials or recount a doctor's visit, I did so sitting at Nobi's sushi bar drinking a little sake and eating a heavenly meal.

We drove back to San Diego that night and waited for Dr. Essner to call with the next opening in his surgery schedule. My rule was I would only allow Dr. Essner to operate when I was his first surgical patient of the day, and we were right around Christmas and New Year's. It took a few days, but my third surgery was scheduled for the first week in January 2005. We drove up the night before, checked into the hotel across from the hospital, then went to Sasabune. This time, I left surgery with a new hockey-stick shaped scar on the right side of my neck below the initial scar line. I also had another JP drain to deal with for a week.

As I thought back to the original diagnosis and sentinel node technique as well as the five-year trial, I concluded a few things about my history. First, I definitely received CancerVax and not a placebo, as the recurrence occurred one year after the study ended. This was only confirmed a few years later when the FDA cancelled the trial after it determined that the vaccine was ineffective, and the study was subsequently "unblinded." Second, I determined that the spot above my ear where the blue dye lit up and Dr. Essner removed tissue during my first surgery represented stray cancer cells that remained dormant while I underwent CancerVax treatment. I figured it took a year for the cells to multiply into a full-grown tumor that became the soft tissue metastases.

I also wondered why the FDA found CancerVax ineffective when my doctors and I believed that it had worked for me. That dichotomy represented the vagaries inherent in the drug discovery process. Just because CancerVax worked for many people including myself, that didn't mean that CancerVax, on a whole, generated significantly better outcomes than did a placebo or existing treatments. All I knew was that if I could have purchased a lifetime supply of CancerVax I would have.

LESSONS LEARNED

• **_Be a strong advocate on your behalf_**

The most important lesson learned throughout these experiences was being a strong advocate on your own behalf. You have to listen to what your body tells you and share that with doctors. You need to inform them and make sure they listen and follow through. Maybe if I had shared more of my history with the dermatologist he would have performed a biopsy and caught the rest of the cancer before it spread further. It doesn't matter anymore, but I did exert more control from then on. My relationship with Dr. Essner enabled me to be very forceful in getting immediate responses and appointments. It is critical to develop those relationships and connections so if you are faced with offices that won't schedule appointments for weeks or days or months out, you can push for quicker action. When I think back to how much territory we covered and how many appointments we had in that one day in December it is aston-ishing. We started at the ENT's office in La Jolla, drove to Santa Monica to see Dr. Essner, drove to Beverly Hills for the CT scan, then back to Santa Monica to see Dr. Essner again and receive results from tests that day, then drove back to San Di-ego. That couldn't have happened had I not become a forceful advocate and had doctors who were amenable to that approach.

CHAPTER EIGHT

What's Next? Let's Try Radiation for $200 Please

As became habit for me, the first thing I did post-surgery (usually the day the stitches were removed) was discuss with Dr. Essner the odds of recurrence, what other steps I could take to prevent recurrence, and whether there were any new clinical trials available.

A quick note about cancer staging. When I was originally diagnosed with the tumor on my scalp, I was considered stage two. When the cancer had spread "locally" to the lymph nodes in the neck, I was restaged to stage three. I thought this recurrence in the same neck region and the parotid gland would make me stage four, but I was still considered stage three. While staging is important in determining treatment options and recovery rates, staging was also important in the clinical trials setting as certain trials were only open to certain stages of cancer.

From Dr. Essner's standpoint, not much had changed in the year since my clinical trial ended. Post-surgery, I was again considered to have "resected" melanoma with no other evidence of disease. Hence, there were still no new clinical trials available. Because the cancer had been in the lymph nodes in the neck region, however, there was a small chance that radiation could help prevent a recurrence. So off I went to meet Dr. Robert Wollman, a radiation oncologist also affiliated with the JWCI.

Dr. Wollman explained that there were various types of radiation. The one he recommended was an extremely high dose that barely penetrated the skin. The hope was that this radiation would kill any stray cells that might have remained post-surgery. He suggested a total of five treatments over two and a half weeks, each of which would last approximately 30 minutes. Most of the time would be spent in setup but the actual radiation would last between five and ten minutes.

I was concerned about the side effects but thankfully, since the total dosage was small, few side effects were expected. It was highly likely I would lose my hair in the area radiated, lose taste buds and have a metallic taste for a while. It was unlikely but possible I could develop sores in the throat around the radiated area. None of these potential side-effects other than the partial hair loss gave me any pause. However, I thought partial hair loss was perfectly manageable for me. If there was any chance this radiation could help prevent recurrence, I was going to do it. My only question was how quickly the doctors would let me start.

I had another problem now, in that I would need to be in Los Angeles for treatment on a Monday, Wednesday, Monday, Wednesday and Monday. I had no desire to drive up each of those days. The solution was my friend, Judy Petraitis, living in Hermosa Beach, who let me stay for free in a spare bedroom at her home. Insurance would not have reimbursed me for the multiple trips and hotels necessary. That network of friends and loved ones became ever more important in my health journey.

With respect to work, Sid only asked that I work if I felt up to it. My laptop enabled me to work virtually anywhere. I committed to putting the time in for necessary tasks and planned to work on other tasks if up to it. Thankfully, my company also had a branch location situated between the radiation oncology office and Judy's home. I worked there a few hours on Monday after treatment, and then again for several hours on Tuesday. I drove home after the treatment on Wednesday. This worked out well for two weeks.

What was radiation like for me? It wasn't so bad. The worst part of the entire course of radiation was the initial set-up session with Dr. Wollman and his assistant. This session lasted three hours and was easily the most painful thing I'd experienced to date. He explained that during the treatment I would need to keep my head perfectly still while lying on my side, so the radiation would only hit the targeted area. The only way to keep me perfectly still was to create a plastic mask that molded to my face in the proper position, that would then be bolted to the table during the actual radiation treatment. While the radiation treatment would only last a few minutes, and the discomfort would be minimal, the setup was not. I had just had my neck fully dissected about two weeks prior and I did not have anywhere near full range of motion. Keeping my head still while lying on my back but tilting my head to the side was extremely uncomfortable to say the least. My head was in a temporary mask locked to the table while they were creating the perfect mask and making adjustments. The strain on my neck muscles was incredibly painful. Only a few times during this three-hour process did Dr. Wollman take a break and unlock my face from the table. This was the most prolonged pain I felt, far exceeding that after three surgeries when at least I was given pain medication. In hindsight I should have asked for a valium or some muscle relaxant to take the edge off while undergoing this planning session.

During the 17 days of treatment and for a short while thereafter the only real side effect was a bitter taste in my mouth when drinking wine or other alcohol. The simple solution was not to drink alcohol for a while. However, the hair loss along the right side of my neck was a bit more problematic. It looked like about a two-inch high by six-inch wide area of my hair had been cut off and it just refused to grow back.

This loss of hair brings up another quirk of my treatments and major point of concern from my wife. I now had two irregular hairless areas on my head. The first was about a two-inch diameter bald spot on the top of my scalp. Because the shape was not quite symmetrical and because the skin looked different from normal head skin (I had a skin graft from my chest that replaced the prior skin), it didn't look like a normal bald spot and a normal progression of hair loss. In fact, the skin was both shiny and looked like an indentation. Anyone looking down on my scalp would notice something not right that would hint at some disease that had caused it. The second chunk on my lower right side of the neck and back of the neck was a bit more challenging as it didn't look anything close to normal.

The question was, did anybody care? Did anybody notice? Did people think about this when they met me and wonder whether I was okay? Did people question my health during professional meetings? The truth is that I never gave too much thought about these issues as I felt 100% healthy and went about my business like there was nothing wrong. Perhaps I had on blinders, but I also believed that most people didn't care about such superficial things. At least in my social and work circles my friends and colleagues knew my health status and didn't care at all what my hair looked like. They were all just happy I was alive and able to be with them. As time went on, however, Suzie began to question this much more and began to exert more pressure to do something to conceal the gaps, including the consideration of some kind of hair transplants.

LESSONS LEARNED

> - *There are many types of radiation therapy and each has different characteristics*
> - *Side effects from radiation differ from one person to the next*

I learned that there are many types of radiation therapy available and they each have different applications across diseases. I also learned that the most important person on the radiation treatment team is the nuclear physicist. It is this individual who, from notes provided by the radiation oncologist and marks and crosses that he draws on your body, writes the computer program that directs the radiation to the designated areas only. I learned that for me the side effects from radiation were minimal and tolerable. I also learned that there is no predicting how radiation will affect you – radiation side effects are quite personalized. Despite best efforts to anticipate how you will react, there is no point to that effort. One just needs to experience it for himself.

CHAPTER NINE

Again, What's Next? Let's Try Clinical Trials for $400 Please

At this point I had resected Stage 3 melanoma and had just finished radiation. I'd become familiar with the www.clinical-trials.gov website and began searching for something new before my next friendly visit with Dr. Essner. There seemed to be quite a number of vaccine trials available at places like UCLA (Los Angeles, CA), USC Norris Cancer Center (Los Angeles, CA), UCSF (San Francisco, CA), MD Anderson (Houston, TX), the Moffitt Cancer Center (Tampa, FL), University of Virginia (Charlottesville, VA), University of Pittsburgh (Pittsburgh, PA), University of Pennsylvania (Philadelphia, PA) and Memorial Sloan Kettering (New York, NY). The trials had various approaches, but most were different combinations of peptides (proteins). Few featured new "drugs" that were different from chemotherapy. The problem was virtually all of the trials required the patient to be HLA A2 positive, which is a blood type most common in Caucasians. I had never heard of HLA blood typing before because it is more commonly associated with matching for organ transplants.

Unfortunately, I was A1 and A3 positive, but A2 negative, which left only one possible trial that by chance happened to be at the USC Norris Cancer Center.

Before I went down that path, my wife and I met with Dr. Steven O'Day, a medical oncologist at the JWCI who would later become my oncologist. I'm grateful that Dr. O'Day made an effort to fit me into his busy schedule on short notice. We met him in his personal office, rather than an exam room, where he was accompanied by a research nurse. I remember dressing up for the meeting in the hopes that he would take me more seriously (normally I would want to be dressed comfortably as possible for medical appointments). I don't even know why I thought looking more professional or well-off would help, but I remember it nonetheless. Dr. O'Day reviewed my medical history and began to explain a clinical trial he was spearheading for a cocktail of drugs known as "biochemotherapy." This cocktail included three forms of chemotherapy (dacarbazine, vinblastine and cisplatin) as well as two immunotherapies – interferon and interleukin-2 ("IL-2"). He told me about one celebrity who had just completed two rounds of this treatment and was showing some promise. The message that I most remember, however, is he believed that biochemotherapy could prolong my survival by several months and maybe a few years. I couldn't believe what I heard. Prior to this consult, every treatment plan was evaluated based on preventing recurrence. This was the first time I'd ever been presented survival statistics. I told him flat out, "with all due respect, I'm not interested in prolonging survival for a few months, I'm interested in preventing recurrence for five years." His response was brutal – "it's my job to give you a dose of reality." Talk about feeling like you've just been kicked in the gut. Here I went through these surgeries and chemotherapy and had no evidence of cancer anywhere in my body, and he was telling me I had to worry about survival.

Prior to this meeting, I don't remember ever considering the possibility I could die from melanoma. Emotionally this was a devastating meeting. I couldn't even fathom that Dr. O'Day was right. Though I was now diagnosed with metastatic melanoma because the cancer had spread and metastasized elsewhere in my body, I was cancer-free at the time. Being cancer-free I was just looking for any available trial that might prevent recurrence. This was the first time I ever felt beat up by a doctor, and I left furious at Dr. O'Day.

For good measure, Dr. O'Day gave us a copy of a research article he had co-written about biochemotherapy. This was my first attempt at reading a peer reviewed article published in a medical journal. Here is the paragraph about survival rates for my diagnosis of metastatic melanoma.

Prompt detection and surgical treatment of early-stage disease can cure most patients. However, the majority of patients with deep primary tumors or tumors that metastasize to regional lymph nodes will succumb to distant metastases. Median survival after the onset of distant metastases is only 6 to 9 months, and the 5-year survival rate is less than 5%.[2]

This was not the type of article I really wanted to read, and not the type of data I wanted to obsess about. Rather, I took the viewpoint that these statistics didn't matter and the only statistic that mattered was me and me alone.

---

[2] Source: Metastatic Melanoma: Chemotherapy to Biochemotherapy
Steven J. O'Day, MD, Christina J. Kim, MD, and Douglas S. Reintgen, MD
Cancer Control, January/February 2002, Vol.9, No.1

My wife and I didn't really need to consult each other about the decision as there was no decision to be made. Certainly, I would try a vaccine trial intended to prevent recurrence before trying biochemotherapy. Dr. O'Day agreed that it would be reasonable for me to join the clinical trial at USC before resorting to biochemotherapy.

We made an appointment with Dr. Jeffrey Weber at USC the following week and took yet another two-hour plus road trip each way. Dr. Weber was another straight-shooting oncologist with a ton of experience. I found him very easy to talk with and easy to understand. I know this is totally irrelevant, but I loved that he wore a bowtie.

He was working on a multi-peptide vaccine that would require me to come to USC every two weeks. He also had a research nurse with him, Jolie Snively, who would become a primary contact. Jolie is one of many amazingly caring and compassionate nurses whom I've met over the years. I qualified for the year-long trial and began in May 2005.

When we checked out after our visit, someone suggested that instead of driving that I could take a two-hour train ride to downtown Los Angeles and then grab a cab for the ten-minute ride to USC. This proved to be a much more comfortable experience for me than driving, especially since I began making these trips alone.

The day my trial began I took the train and it was so easy. Before I could begin the trial, however, I had to undergo a laboratory process called "leukapheresis." This process entailed having my blood drawn from one arm, fed through a machine that spun out the white blood cells, then fed back into my other arm. I had to remain alert for the entire two-hour process and keep pumping my arm to ensure proper blood flow. The purpose for the leukapheresis was to be able to measure changes in my white blood cells from pre-trial to post-trial. I remember the feeling of blood pumping back in as it was unexpectedly quite cold, and this feeling was only in the left arm.

Having completed the leukapheresis, I walked over to the treatment area of the Norris Cancer Center. The peptide vaccine was to be injected subcutaneously into my thighs and then I would be able to go home. The "aha" moment came when Jolie brought in two bags of ice for my thighs. She explained that the injections would be painful, and the ice was to numb the injection site. I don't know how athletes routinely ice their muscles but having two bags of ice on my legs for twenty minutes was not particularly comfortable. On the other hand, I would have regretted not having the ice as it really did help to deaden, but not eliminate, the pain from the injections. Thirty minutes in total at the clinic was not much time at all, and I was looking forward to relaxing on the train ride back to San Diego.

I began this treatment during softball and baseball season and I remember going directly from the train station to the field for whichever one of my kids had a game that afternoon. The other parents knew what I was going through and were always very comforting. The pain from the injections subsided by game time but the injections did leave bumps that lasted for at least a week while the vaccine was dissipating into my body. To this day, I sometimes feel those bumps in my thighs, although I know they aren't there. Phantom pain, itching and bumps just goes with the territory I guess.

This treatment continued through August. I began to feel a very tiny nodule in my right neck and showed it to Dr. Weber before my next injections on the Friday before Labor Day. The nodule was so tiny and deep under the skin that I wasn't sure he would have noticed it during his routine examination of the lymph nodes around the neck. After the injections he came back and performed a "punch" biopsy, quickly and painlessly removed the tiny nodule, and sent it to pathology. He said the pathology report wouldn't be available before Tuesday, but I could tell by the look in his eyes that he was quite worried that the melanoma returned.

Aside from calling my wife with the news, I called my boss Sid, who was also a dear friend. Sid said without hesitation, don't worry about work. Just work on getting healthy. That was just what I needed to hear before jumping on the train back to San Diego. Not a day goes by that I don't feel fortunate for having Sid as my boss. His compassion and care made a huge difference in my life and how I thought about leadership. That weekend was the longest weekend I could remember. I was certain of the results and by the end of Tuesday, the bad feelings were confirmed. I had cancer again.

LESSONS LEARNED

> - *It is critical to have a second advocate with you at key appointments*
> - *Don't spare any details from your doctors and nurses*

It is worth repeating how important it is to be your own advocate. But it is also critical to have a second person with you at every consultation. As patients, we are too invested in wanting to say what we feel we need to say, and often miss hearing details because our focus is on talking. We are also scared and very short on patience. This is very common and not something to feel bad about. It is just a simple fact that our listening skills are not so keen when doctors are presenting very detailed information about medical conditions and prospective treatments. Always have someone else with you and if possible, make sure it is the same person each time. Continuity is also important in this respect.

I also learned that no detail should ever be spared from your doctor or nurses. Was my nodule so tiny that it could have been anything and disappeared before the next appointment? I suppose so, but why take the risk? When you are undergoing treatment, every detail, no matter how small, might matter. And every day of waiting for cancer to grow could magnify your problem. I developed a very simple philosophy that if I needed surgery, I wanted it done as quickly as possible. No waiting. No consulting with others. No scouring the internet for unreliable but terrifying information. Get the cancer out of my body as quickly as humanly possible and let's move on to the next option.

CHAPTER TEN

What and When Do You Tell the Kids

What had we been telling our children for all this time? Of course, we didn't tell them anything before my first surgery because Sam was turning four and Jordan wasn't even two. There was nothing to explain. There wasn't much to tell them during the course of the CancerVax trial either as I was just making day trips to Los Angeles. But things changed with the first recurrence and surgery number three. Sam was ten years old and Jordan was seven and a half. They were aware something was up when we arranged for their grandparents to pick them up from school the day we made the unplanned trip to Los Angeles to see Dr. Essner to get the MRI and CT scans.

On our drive home that evening from Los Angeles we decided that we needed to tell Sam and Jordan what was going on. But we didn't tell them that night as we got home late. Also, and more importantly, we reached out to a family therapist we knew. Then we read a book the next day (I wish I could remember which) that talked about how to tell your children about cancer. Time was of the essence because we were scheduling surgery as soon as possible.

I remember sitting down with Sam and Jordan on the couch to explain that I had cancer and needed to have surgery. I could see the worried look in my children's eyes as soon as I asked them to sit down for an important talk. This look never gets any easier to see. We were fairly detailed in explaining that I had skin cancer that arose from too much sun exposure as a child that only affected me later in life. We told them that I would be in a hospital overnight and that I would need to recover at home for a few days. We told them about the JP drain I would have so they wouldn't be surprised. And we told them that I expected to be 100% quickly. We didn't promise the cancer would be gone for good but promised that if it ever happened again I would do whatever it takes to get healthy. We explained that after surgery I would be looking for any kind of medicine to prevent the cancer from coming back. We also had to explain in terms they could understand that skin cancer isn't hereditary. That meant simply that they wouldn't get the same cancer just because they were our children.

I don't remember Sam and Jordan having too many questions as they mostly just listened and needed time to process. But Jordan did ask "Why did God let this happen to you?" I didn't have a good answer as I don't believe there is a good one. Or, at least, I don't know that there is a right one. Rather, I turned the attention away from God and back to the environment and sun exposure. I explained that we didn't wear sunscreen as children. Indeed, as teens, we put on tanning oil and relished that first burn of the summer that turned into a deep tan later. This became the start of the important ritual of making sure Sam and Jordan wore sunscreen when they were outdoors.

It was always easy for me to take the positive approach because that's how my brain was wired. I never felt sorrow or anger as I didn't have time for those emotions. I didn't think about "why did this happen to me." I thought back to the book *Prepare for Surgery – Heal Faster* and remembered that eliminating as much stress as possible and being relaxed increased my T-cell count and ability to fight disease. I wanted to live and see my children grow up. I wanted to surround myself with positive emotions and people. Consequently, I was always passionate about fighting, and Sam and Jordan knew that.

Coming home after surgery was a blessing, more so this time because Sam and Jordan were there to comfort me as well. They were attentive and aware of how to touch and hug me without risk of popping stitches or pulling out the JP drain. The warmth of family makes recovery much easier and sweeter, and of course enabled me to stay positive throughout.

When I was about to begin clinical trial number two, we had another conversation as I needed to explain that process and why I would be late for their baseball and softball games. As expected, Sam and Jordan were both glad we shared the truth, a little nervous because I was having more treatment, and optimistic because that was the primary emotion I shared.

LESSONS LEARNED

> • *There is no formula that tells you when to share your cancer diagnosis with your children*
> • *Always provide your children with other adults to speak with and share their feelings*

I don't believe there is a magic formula about what or when to tell kids about your illness. I think it is helpful to seek the guidance of therapists or spiritual advisors who might know your children. But I do know that the truth is what stands out. Children are nothing if not observant. They see fear and they see hope. They see pain and they see ease. They feel what you feel and watch you and your reactions for cues on how they should act. And they have really good BS detectors, so don't think you can outsmart them.

The other advice I would give here is to make sure children know that they can always talk to you, ask questions and get the facts. I also think you should make sure that they know that you will provide someone for them to talk with if they are ever worried about sharing with you. That is, make available another adult, a therapist, a priest, a rabbi, a grandparent, or anyone with whom they feel comfortable talking openly. Children must know that your love is unwavering and that you support all of their emotional and talking needs. These vary with age and maturity, of course, but never lose sight of the fact that they need an outlet, and that outlet might not be you.

CHAPTER ELEVEN

Surgery Number Four (September 2005)

Back to Los Angeles we went for surgery number four. This time, Dr. Essner was going to redo the right lymphadenectomy along the same scar line as surgery number two. Since I'd arranged to be his first surgery of the day, we needed to stay in a hotel near the hospital the night before. Since driving to Los Angeles late afternoon is a mistake due to traffic, we left just after lunch and found a good spot for dinner (Sasabune was closed that night). Again, I was thankful to have my in-laws in San Diego who watched our children.

The nights before surgery were never relaxing or easy, even though I'd become accustomed to them and learned how to meditate or otherwise calm myself down. I had to stop eating at least eight hours in advance of my morning appointment (we were due at the hospital between 6:00 am and 6:30 am) so late-night snacking or drinks were not allowed. I'd made a habit of trying to read in bed while listening to relaxing music. Conversation with Suzie was also challenging since the tension and anxiety was high. Sleep was not really restful, and my body anticipated the need to wake up early for surgery.

As I've mentioned before, Dr. Essner is considered one of the finest surgical oncologists in the United States and is extremely precise and thorough. He estimated this surgery to last three hours. Unfortunately for my wife who was waiting patiently in the hospital, this surgery lasted almost five hours. This is another reason I insisted on being his first surgical patient in the morning. Once surgery was complete, I was rolled to the recovery room where it took me at least an hour to wake-up and become alert. This was not 100% alertness like I could read or drive, but at least alert enough to go to the bathroom, ask for a drink of water and ask for a cracker or ice cream.

It is very important for recovery and leaving the hospital as quickly as possible to urinate and eat without problems. The sooner I did so the better. My healing statements that I gave to Dr. Essner and the anesthesiologist prior to surgery (I did so each time) included that I would pee freely and be hungry for ice cream. I don't know whether these really helped but my body was able to recover quite quickly, and I was able to pee and eat within hours. Once I was able to do so I was moved from recovery to a hospital room for the night.

Dr. Essner came to check on me first thing in the morning, making sure the incision looked good and that the JP drain was working properly. As all was in order, I asked to be released as soon as possible. Did I say I hate being in hospitals? It's harder to say which I valued more, wanting to get into the hospital for surgery as soon as possible or leaving as quickly as possible post-surgery. But I think both were important traits and I was thankful for my ability to focus on those goals and actually make both happen. Maybe it's a function of age and general health, but I believe my brain works in conjunction with my body to help me recovery so quickly. Back to San Diego we went and another two hours on the freeway.

Surgery was Tuesday, I was home Wednesday, and my sister-in-law was getting married Saturday. Thankfully, Dr. Essner only put steri-tape over the stiches instead of a large bandage. Late Saturday morning, as we were preparing for the wedding, a most extraordinary thing happened that I will never forget. My wife had a group appointment for hair and make-up in a small salon across the street from an old friend's office. I needed the fresh air, so I accompanied her. My friend had several golden retrievers and I was looking forward to sitting on the couch with her and just catching up. After a quick but light hug, I sat down. No sooner had I sat down than Montana, the female golden retriever, jumped up slowly, inched her way directly adjacent to me, sat straight up, rested her paw on my thigh as if to say "you're going to be ok," and put the side of her face right next to my scar. Montana didn't budge for the entire hour I sat in the office. Montana puts the words "therapy dog" in "therapy dog." So, while my intent was to catch up with my friend, which I did, the end result was receiving the most intensive, loving therapy ever, and from a dog no less. When I need to think of happy places, this is one of the first pictures that comes to my mind.

LESSONS LEARNED

> - *Ask for a prescription for sleeping pills if you are unable to fall asleep without help pre-surgery*

Since sleep doesn't come easily before surgery but is needed to put your body into its most rested and relaxed state, I learned to ask for a sleeping pill prescription. I also learned that the reason hospitals ask you to arrive so early is more a function of managing all the pre-op appointments than the actual time needed to prep you. Once you become comfortable with the process (I hate saying this), and once you know that the nurses don't have challenges getting IV needles into your arm (or hand), and once you realize how long you wait in pre-op before rolling you into the operating room, you can adjust your wake time so you don't arrive until the end of your appointment window. Unless you are running late for your surgery, you are likely to wait for other patients to be called before you anyway.

CHAPTER TWELVE

What's Next (Seriously, Again), or Second Opinions for $600 Please (October 2005)

I felt I needed a second opinion on what to do next to prevent yet another recurrence. Up to this point, I had only seen doctors in Los Angeles and sensed that I might get other ideas from oncologists at different cancer locations. I ask Dr. Essner for two referrals. He recommended two oncologists with excellent reputations at world-renowned cancer centers. Armed with their names and phone numbers, I began the process of scheduling essentially back-to-back appointments across the country.

When booking these types of appointments with oncologists who are also noted researchers in their field, I knew to ask for their research nurses, not just scheduling nurses. The research nurses had a better understanding of my current condition and past treatments to facilitate a productive appointment. Moreover, I needed to share with them the latest scans, pathology reports and treatment regimens. Only with this information was I be able to schedule an appointment. I also needed to have the referral from another high-level oncologist to get a timely response. That's just the way it worked. Blind calling took longer.

After multiple phone calls, I was able to book appointments about a week apart. My next step was to book flights and hotels. I learned that our east coast destination was not very easy to get to from San Diego, so we needed to fly in and out of Los Angeles, requiring a drive from San Diego and parking our car at the airport. We found a hotel not far from the hospital location enabling us to make the 11:00 a.m. appointment without needing to drive very far.

This was probably the first trip I'd taken in my life that wasn't for business or pleasure. What does one think about doing in a day and a half in a new city when the primary purpose is a medical visit? Well, there is not enough time to be a true tourist and certainly no time to drive all around town and wander around new neighborhoods. We decided to look into fun restaurants in hip neighborhoods because we only had tourist time for two dinners and a lunch.

Being burger fans, we went to the highest rated burger joint the night we arrived. It was a pretty lively place in a fun neighborhood and this was just the kind of meal we needed before seeing a new oncologist. Morning came, and we ate a very light breakfast as we had found a really good lunch spot. Unfortunately, things didn't turn out quite like we planned. When we arrived at the hospital, we were very quickly moved to an examination room and I was asked to strip and put on a gown. In my experience this was very unusual, but I followed the directions. Well, we waited and waited and waited for three hours with but one knock on the door from a nurse saying the doctor would see us soon. Sitting in a cold examination room in a gown is not my idea of a pleasant experience. I had never before been asked to strip for an oncology consultation but instead was asked to remove my shirt when the doctor arrived. So not only was I cold but very uncomfortable physically and emotionally. I'd have been much happier sitting in the waiting area than this situation.

Finally, the doctor arrived. Much to my surprise (and anger), he didn't even apologize for being late or keeping us waiting. At this point, this University was 0 for 2 in my book on patient experience. The doctor looked at my file quickly and the first words out of his mouth were "your scans are out of date Mr. Engel, so I presume you have more disease and I am now calling you stage four." His second sentence began his litany of treatments he could offer me (two or three I think, as I had a hard time listening at this point). The entire appointment lasted only about ten minutes, which was not at all what we had expected after traveling cross country and waiting for three hours.

I was devastated, miserable, hungry and extremely pissed off. First of all, how could my scans be out of date when I had spoken to his research nurse at least five times and she knew the exact date of my last scans? If she knew they would be out of date, why wouldn't she have told me to get new scans or have me take them at their hospital the day of or day before the appointment? I'm a pretty good patient and do what I'm told. This was astonishing to me. Then, for the doctor to just lay out all these drug protocols with no real discussion? Given the way I was treated, even if he had a reasonable option there was no way I was going to fly to this city on a regular basis when this was how they treated me.

I had another appointment scheduled in Houston the next week and I did not want to experience that again, so the first

thing we did before heading to find food was to call Dr. Essner
to explain what happened and ask him to order fresh scans. I
would have ordered scans myself, but patients are unable to
make those kind of orders (especially if you want insurance to
pay). Thankfully for me I had Dr. Essner's cell phone and I was
able to reach him in Seattle where he was attending a medical
conference. I provided him the name and phone number of fa-
cilities in San Diego where I had scans before and he
immediately went to work ordering fresh scans for the day after
I returned to San Diego.

We were starving and not in a very good mood, so lunch
wasn't really an option. It was now about 3:30 and we decided
to go to one of the city's hottest restaurants where we sat down
at the bar and immediately ordered a cocktail. It took the restaurant a little while to get food going so I'm pretty sure we
were two or three drinks in before food came. We weren't in
much of a talking mood and I can say that this was not a memorable experience. We just wanted to drown our sorrows at this
point and get back to the hotel as we had an early morning flight
back home. Back in the hotel room, we both threw up from all
of the alcohol we consumed on an empty stomach. I'm sure the
emotional day made matters on our stomachs worse. This was
probably the most dejected I'd ever been in my journey so far.

The flight to Los Angeles and the two-hour drive to San Diego the next day weren't much better. We got home, unpacked
and took much needed showers. I needed to make sure I was
clear for getting my CT scan and brain/neck MRI the next day.
I couldn't eat before the scans and just wanted to get through
them as quickly as possible. I'd been through this routine a few
times before, so I was pretty comfortable with the process of
driving from one facility to the next and just powering through.

I had my favorite mellow music to listen to while waiting and just made the best of it.

The next week we were off to Houston and the M.D. Anderson Cancer Center. It was only a two-hour flight to Houston from San Diego and this experience couldn't have been any more different than the prior experience. M.D. Anderson is such a large complex that they have an on-site hotel for patients and family. Many patients spend multiple days for treatment, so this hotel was extremely convenient.

Unlike our last trip, where we knew no one, Suzie's ex-tennis partner and her husband lived in Houston. We made plans to visit them at their home late afternoon and then they took us to a lovely dinner in an old church converted into a restaurant. We had been on pins and needles ever since the last trip and seeing them was just the antidote we needed. Being with old friends, catching up, avoiding the medical discussions and just being free of worry for a few hours enabled me to get a decent night's sleep for the first time in weeks.

We arrived at the melanoma center desk to check-in and not five minutes after completing the paperwork were walked back to the exam room. An assistant oncologist entered within ten minutes and she conducted a preliminary exam. I handed her the film of the scans I had brought with from San Diego and the senior oncologist, Dr. Hwu, came in about ten minutes later. I wasn't asked to strip to a gown, which made me much more comfortable. I was examined again by Dr. Hwu. Unfortunately, he confirmed from the scans that the oncologist from a city to which I never wanted to return was correct and the cancer had returned. I had multiple tumors in the lymph nodes on both sides of the neck, some in my chest and a suspicious spot in my right armpit.

Dr. Hwu recommended an immunotherapy treatment option call high-dose interleukin-2. The protocol for this treatment required a trip to Houston once every three weeks for at least five treatments and I would need to spend one night in the hospital. At that point in time, high-dose IL-2 was considered a front-line treatment for metastatic melanoma even though there was very high toxicity associated with the treatment. Side effects included fever and chills, diarrhea, nausea, low blood counts, lowered blood pressure, changes in liver functions and swelling of the face, ankles or legs. However, based upon the professionalism of Dr. Hwu and the M.D. Anderson staff, we left feeling convinced that I would begin high-dose IL-2 treatment at M.D. Anderson.

As soon as we landed back in San Diego that night I called Dr. Essner to tell him about the visit and our decision. What I heard from him was not expected at all. He told me that under no circumstances should I begin high-dose IL-2. He felt that it was old science and that the chances for success were extremely limited. More importantly, he said that Dr. O'Day was getting ready to report much stronger data from his biochemotherapy therapy regimen that would indicate I should adopt that protocol. I was extremely surprised by this response since he recommended I see Dr. Hwu in the first place. I called Dr. Weber at USC the next day to ask his opinion. Dr. Weber was equally emphatic that I shouldn't try high-dose IL-2 and that I should try biochemotherapy. Moreover, and against his best financial interests, he recommended that I have Dr. O'Day treat me, even though he was himself capable. He believed Dr. O'Day had more experience with biochemotherapy. He also thought the continuity of care at St. John's Hospital and the JWCI (and now The Angeles Clinic, a spin-off of the medical oncology group[3] from the JCWI) would be beneficial to me. I really respected Dr. Weber for that and am grateful that I have been with doctors who truly put my health needs first.

LESSONS LEARNED

> - ***Keep several copies of all pathology reports, lab results, scan, clinical trial consent forms, etc. to share with other doctors***
> - ***Develop a strong relationship with your primary oncologist or care provider***

One of the most important lessons learned here is to make sure you create a detailed personal file with copies of all pathology reports, scans, blood work, treatment protocols, clinical trial consent forms, and any other documents related to your health history. Whenever you get scans, make sure you don't leave without three copies on CDs (although this may be less important today if doctors are able to access digital files). You need to always keep one copy for yourself and have at least two available to bring to appointments. The reality is that every good doctor wants to see the images herself and not just read clinical and pathology reports. And they typically want to go over complete history as changes that occur in time are meaningful in developing and recommending treatment options.

Make sure you develop a strong relationship with your primary oncologist. I'm not sure Dr. Essner would have answered my call in Seattle if we didn't have that kind of relationship

---

[3] Dr. Essner was a surgical oncologist who didn't administer or advise on chemotherapies or other regimens. Dr. Weber, Dr. Hwu and Dr. O'Day were medical oncologists who didn't operate.

where he knew exactly what was going on and had a genuine concern for my welfare. Our bond was really one of the most significant advantages I had in navigating through the various processes. I trusted Dr. Essner with my life many times and he never let me down. And he wasn't afraid to recommend that I get treated elsewhere if there was a better option. I developed the same kind of relationship with Dr. Weber, albeit over a shorter time span, and he exhibited the same interest in my care. The fact that he would advise me over the phone instead of insisting that I come in for an appointment to discuss the options speaks volumes to his integrity. It is very rare that a doctor will share opinions outside of the clinic and I was fortunate to be able to rely on my doctors at all times of the day.

CHAPTER THIRTEEN

Clinical Trial Number Three: Biochemotherapy (November 2005)

Biochemotherapy was a nasty cocktail consisting of three chemotherapy drugs and two immunotherapy drugs. Each was highly toxic in its own right. Put them together and oncologists concocted the perfect storm of toxicity. Or, to use a well-known phrase, let's throw everything but the kitchen sink and see what sticks.

So here was the protocol I embarked upon. The biochemotherapy induction regimen included cisplatin, vinblastine, dacarbazine, decrescendo interleukin-2 (IL-2), and interferon alfa-2b. These were administered in a hospital every day for five days. I would enter the hospital on Friday and leave on Tuesday. On Wednesday I was required to go to Dr. O'Day's office for an IV-infusion of liquid nutrients. When I went home, a home care nurse would visit to establish the IV-infusion for four more days. I then had ten days to begin eating what I could before going in to the hospital again. Each cycle was 21 days.

First things first. To facilitate such intensive treatments, Dr. Essner operated early that Friday morning and inserted a "portacath" in my left chest. In scientific terms, a "port" consisted of a reservoir compartment (the portal) that has a silicone bubble for needle insertion (the septum), with an attached plastic tube (the catheter). The device was surgically inserted under the skin in the upper chest and appeared as a bump under my skin. It required no special maintenance and was completely internal, so swimming and bathing were not a problem. The catheter ran from the portal and was surgically inserted into a vein (usually the jugular vein, subclavian vein, or superior vena cava). Ideally, the catheter terminated in the superior vena cava, just upstream of the right atrium. This position allowed infused agents to be spread throughout the body quickly and efficiently. The following pictures help visualize the portacath. The first diagram shows the connections, the second photograph the actual device outside of the body being punctured and the third is what it looked like under the skin.

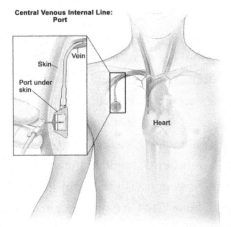

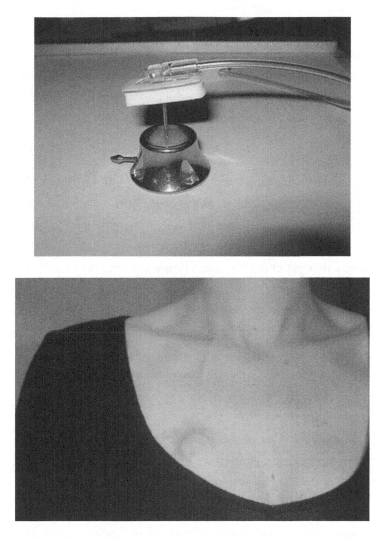

In layman terms, they put a big collection spot under my chest so instead of having to continuously stick needles in my arms, they could simply put a needle through my skin directly into this catheter that enabled the nurses to both push the drugs intravenously and withdraw blood. Because of the large volume of fluids I was going to have injected, I essentially had a "double-wide" portacath. I have to say that it was much more tolerable, although a little odd of a feeling, to have needles go directly through the skin rather than inserted in your arms. Moreover, once the nurse inserted the two needles before starting treatment, I didn't need to be stuck again for the entire five days.

Once the portacath was surgically implanted, my next stop was patient admission to a special oncology floor. But not just any oncology floor. Biochemotherapy was so toxic and required such intensive care that only specially trained nurses helped biochemotherapy patients and they could only be assigned two patients at a time. Sounds crazy, doesn't it? But that's the situation. I was fortunate to be admitted by a very sweet, older nurse who was very forthright. She told me not to bother asking for hospital meals because I would just throw them up anyway. She advised me to smoke marijuana if I could tolerate it as marijuana would be extremely helpful in managing side effects. And she told me to just keep my spirits up as best I could.

For your reading pleasure let me share the science on potential side effects straight out of a medical journal article detailing the biochemotherapy regimen.

Biochemotherapy patients can be managed on inpatient oncology units without routine intensive monitoring or vasopressor support; however, all patients experience constitutional symptoms including fever, chills, rigors, myalgias, fatigue, anorexia, and headache to varying degrees. Gastrointestinal symptoms of nausea, vomiting, and diarrhea are also prominent. Hematologic toxicity is expected and includes leukopenia, anemia, and thrombocytopenia. Neutropenia and anemia can be well managed with empiric growth factor support. Cumulative thrombocytopenia is managed with dose reductions of chemotherapy. Intermediate-dose IL-2-specific tox-icity includes varying degrees of capillary leak syndrome with hypotension, fluid retention, and third-spacing, pul-monary congestion and reversible end-organ dysfunction.[4]

In layman terms this means that the treatment would totally suck, and I was going to feel sick as a dog. I would be so sick from the drugs that I needed to take a bunch of other drugs to offset the side effects. Over the course of three days my body would balloon from all of the fluids pumped into my system that I would need diuretics days four and five just to get myself back to normal. My body would turn lobster red from all this crap and my skin would dry up and crack. I would need to con-tinuously rub Eucerin all over my body to prevent body sores. Sounded like a lot of fun to me.

I had been given a preview of all this from Dr. O'Day, in-cluding the scientific research from which I quoted above. When my family in San Diego asked what they could do to help, I was pretty specific. I figured that I would I hate the sounds of the hospital (I'd been in many times before for my surgeries), so I asked for a portable speaker into which I could plug my iPod. I then loaded my iPod with all of my jazz, new age and mellow music, and created hours-long playlists. In hindsight, this was one of the best things I did.

I also figured that I would want one good meal before be-ginning treatment as I knew I wouldn't be eating for at least six if not ten days. I asked my friend Ilan to bring me a pastrami sandwich from Langer's Deli near downtown Los Angeles. For

---

[4] Source: Metastatic Melanoma: Chemotherapy to Biochemotherapy
Steven J. O'Day, MD, Christina J. Kim, MD, and Douglas S. Reintgen, MD
Cancer Control, January/February 2002, Vol.9, No.1

those of you not from LA, many foodies consider this the best pastrami sandwich west of New York. I certainly did. And boy did it taste good as I was getting settled into my hospital bed. If you could picture thick, hand carved warm pastrami on double-baked rye bread with a crunchy crust you'd have it about right. My mouth watered just thinking of this sandwich. Shortly after eating the sandwich and settling in, my wife drove back to San Diego to be with the kids only to return on Tuesday when I was to be released.

For those of you who don't eat meat, you won't appreciate this, and you might even be offended by the picture above. I understand and don't mean to offend you. Instead, picture yourself savoring your favorite food, whatever it is. Think that this would be your last meal for ten days. That's the feeling you need to conjure to understand how I felt. I know that you know how good that tastes in your mouth.

Now, picture the treatment beginning. I've got two IV lines into my portacath, one with saline and other nutrients, and the other for the drugs. First, the nurse pumped some Benadryl to calm me down and prevent (ha ha ha) nausea and infection.

Next came chemotherapy, one at a time. They were delivered in dark yellow bags so everyone in the hospital knew not to touch them without wearing special gloves. These drugs were even toxic to the nurses if not handled properly. It was a little eerie and a lot scary. Next came IL-2, and the rigors. I didn't know what rigors were, but I learned fast. I started to shake uncontrollably, as if my body was freezing. I asked the nurse for a warm blanket. Only that didn't work. So, I asked for another warm blanket. And that didn't work. So I asked for a third. And that didn't work. So, I asked for a fourth. Maybe that worked. Or I needed a fifth. Now, I was slowly calming down and the shaking had stopped. But I now had a fever from the five warm blankets. Next came the Tylenol to control the fever. Following IL-2 I was administered interferon that causes instant nausea. And I mean instant. And the nurses didn't even warn me how instant instant was. Before I knew it, my Langer's pastrami was coming back up. I can say with all seriousness that pastrami does not feel good going the other direction. It was downright disgusting and left a lingering bad taste in my mouth. Unfortunately for me, this lingering bad taste prevented me from eating another pastrami sandwich for at least a year after starting biochemotherapy. But don't worry my carnivore friends – I learned to enjoy pastrami again.

So much for day one on biochemotherapy. Now came the night time, when I was not really allowed to sleep. Why, you might ask? Because the nurse needed to wake me every two hours to take vital signs. What else disrupted my sleep in the oncology ward? The sounds of patients screaming or moaning in pain echoing down the halls. Oh, I really hated that sound. Why? Because I was always positive and knew that I had a lot to live for. I was going to fight with all my might. I couldn't bear listening to others' pain. Thankfully for me I had my trusty iPod and portable speaker. Unfortunately for me there was no room for the iPod next to my bed, so it was located on a counter across the room and I needed a nurse to turn it on. What's a little funny now looking back is that I had to teach the nurse how to use an iPod as iPods were relatively new back in 2005. But since I had a seven-hour playlist of all my mellow new agey stuff, she only had to get it going once at night.

Day two was not much different from day one. At this point I want to share a funny story about how I got Dr. O'Day's cell phone number. Recall that I considered it very important to get my oncologist's cell phone number if I needed something urgently. This proved very important to me when I was back East for that second opinion. I suppose I could have just asked Dr. O'Day for his number, but I didn't. However, I had heard from the nurses that he had a great ring tone – the Notre Dame fight song. When he came to check on me in the morning I asked him to play the ring tone for me. Of course, he had no clue how to find it on his phone as back then phones were much dumber and someone else had added the ring tone for him. My solution – I told Dr. O'Day to give me his number and I'd call him. When his phone rang I would hear it. Simple as that, I had his cell phone number. I never abused having that number and only called him on it once over the next two years.

Back to treatment. The drugs needed to be administered in the same order and I was grateful for the Benadryl drip to begin the proceedings. Nighty night I went for a couple of hours. But then the IL-2 and the rigors came with a vengeance. I got no relief from that and again faced the same routine of blankets and Tylenol. Then the dreaded interferon. This time, I didn't have any food in my system to throw up. Also, my nurse and I talked about the importance of the following message: push interferon very slowly. Interferon wasn't on a drip like the chemotherapies but was injected directly into the catheter below the saline drip. This was a message I learned to repeat as a mantra with each nurse every morning – push slowly, push very slowly. There was no rush and I didn't need to get nauseous.

About now I was beginning to feel some of the other side effects, like the bloated body, red skin and diarrhea. Not run-of-the-mill diarrhea, of course. But the uncontrollable kind that hits you in bed before you can even ask a nurse to help you to the toilet. It is times like these where I began to appreciate how difficult it must be for nurses to deal with patients like me on a regular basis. Diarrhea in bed probably happened two to three times a day. This unpleasant feeling of helplessness never disappeared, but, as the days wore on, I became numb to that feeling.

Unfortunately for me I began to develop another side effect that had my doctor quite worried. My albumin levels dropped precipitously, indicating my kidneys were not working properly. This condition required a new doctor – a nephrologist. I can recall the concerned look on Dr. O'Day's face as he was consulting with the nephrologist. They decided to modify the doses of the biochemotherapy to bring my kidney functions back to normal. Ultimately, the albumin levels still weren't where they needed to be on Tuesday and I was required to spend an extra night in the hospital.

Day three was more of the same, although now I'd put on over 10 pounds of water weight and I was truly a balloon. This was quite uncomfortable on top of everything else. But the reality was I was on so many drugs I couldn't even recognize what was going on. I drifted in and out of sleep pretty much all day and night. Meanwhile, George Winston kept playing in the background, dulling my senses to the outside noises.

Did I have visitors during my five-day hospital stay after my wife drove home? One of things that made it easy for her to drive home was that my parents were still in Los Angeles and my mother visited often during the day. My sister Deborah also lived in Los Angeles and visited either with or without my mom. We didn't talk much as I was pretty much dead to the world during the treatment. But it was comforting having them in the room and having my dad visit at night after work. My friends Jamie and Ilan also visited every couple of days, even if just for a few minutes. Although they never told me, I could tell that it was equally uncomfortable for my visitors to see me in a hospital bed with multiple bags hanging on the rail, half-asleep, beet red and bloated, and just plain miserable. But they came anyway because it was important for me to have that connection. That love was so important to my mental condition and spirit, yet I was never really alert enough to convey how much it meant to me. Maybe this book is my way of sharing some of that appreciation.

Day four was the peak of my bloatedness, so the nurse began to administer Lasix, a diuretic that basically made me pee more often than I'd like to share. And because I couldn't get out of the bed by myself, I began to feel self-conscious again about asking for help every half hour. I guess that is why the nurses could only handle two biochemotherapy patients at a time. It's not just the time and care it takes to administer each of the drugs, but it's all the time and heavy lifting required to manage the side effects, taking patients to the bathroom, cleaning patients after making a mess in the bed, changing the sheets, moving patients back into the bed, fetching hot blanket after hot blanket, coming back with more Tylenol, etc. etc. etc. These nurses were saints who I learned to love like family.

Day five was the decrescendo of the IL-2 and the last of the biochemotherapy drugs. But alas, as I said before, I wasn't able to leave that day because of low albumin levels. My wife spent the night in the hotel room that we were to share together before my appointment for IV-infusion in Dr. O'Day's office at The Angeles Clinic the next day. That night Suzie began a new routine to communicate with family and friends. She wrote an email update on my condition that was similar in content to a blog post. She tried to inject humor where possible and I came to learn that people loved reading her posts. I wished I had kept them as they would have made a fun appendix to this book. I was released on the morning of day six and I was so relieved to be in a hotel bed instead of the hospital bed. The Ambrose Hotel in Santa Monica became a new home away from home for me.

Day seven was when I first met two of the kindest, gentlest, funniest, most compassionate chemotherapy nurses in the world, Cathy Webb and Secela Evans. Cathy and Secela essentially ran the infusion room which consisted of four reclining chairs in a large room with two recliners in a smaller adjacent room. There were small screens between recliners, but I was essentially in an open room full of other patients, their family (most patients had one caregiver with them) and up to four nurses. This IV infusion was just fluid and nutrients that lasted about an hour. Following a quick check-up by Dr. O'Day, we were able to drive home. I was never more thankful to see my children than that afternoon.

What was astonishing to me was how sensitive my children were to my condition. Intuitively, they knew how hard they could hug and hold me, and how physically close to get to express their love. And this was the kind of love that reminded me every day of what I was fighting for. I craved seeing Sam and Jordan, hearing their voices, sitting next to them on the couch, feeling their love, giving them gentle kisses. There is nothing I wouldn't do to make sure I was alive to see them grow up. Even going through up to three more rounds of biochemotherapy.

Day eight came and we received the first visit from the home health nurse. She brought gifts – IV-bags to administer twice a day for three to four days. She inserted a new catheter into the portacath and taught my wife how to hook up the IV bag. Suzie was not particularly comfortable with this process, which is understandable, but she ultimately became very skilled at hooking up my twice-daily feedings.

What else did I do while I was at home, visibly and appreciably weaker than when I went into the hospital? I tried to take walks around the neighborhood as often as possible. At least five times a day I ventured out the front door and walked further and further. I happened to have a wonderful neighbor Jennifer who worked out of her house and would accompany me on many of my walks to make sure I didn't fall. Her husband was a cardiologist who also looked in on me daily to make sure I was doing okay. I never really thought I'd fall on my walks, but I enjoyed the company nonetheless.

What about eating normal food? I'd read all the stories about how chemotherapy would destroy my appetite and taste buds. Each chemotherapy has its own characteristics, but in my case, the combination did indeed kill all appetite and taste. About the only thing I could tolerate was a mint-chip ice cream shake from Baskin-Robbins. My wife went once or twice a day to the local store to pick up a shake in hopes that I would eat the whole cup. Nutritionally speaking, ice cream shakes are not very healthy, but the flip side was that my body desperately needed calories to build my strength up for the next round in the hospital. It turns out that ice cream shakes were actually good for me! This eating habit continued during my two weeks at home.

Sometimes I'd have friends bring me the shake and come visit instead of sending Suzie. I knew this was hard for most of my friends to do as they worked during the day. But I really appreciated the visits and change of pace. This is a good stopping point to discuss friends and how they react to cancer and post-treatment visits. I found out very quickly that there were some people who were just not comfortable at all seeing me in pajamas or sweat pants, obviously exhausted, weak and at my worst physical condition. They came by once and never came back. Others just viewed me as a friend in need and gave me all the attention I desired.

LESSONS LEARNED

> - *Become comfortable asking for help and be specific in what help you need*
> - *Don't take it personally when family or friends can't really handle your condition*

I think I incorporated most of the lessons I learned throughout these 21 days into the body of the chapter. But a very important lesson is you must become comfortable asking for exactly what you need. In my case, I asked Jennifer for a hand when I wanted to take a longer walk around the neighborhood. I asked Dave Altman to come visit and bring a shake when I needed company. I asked Suzie's aunts who were great chefs to make meals, so she didn't need to cook. You see, many people will say "tell me what I can do," but if you're not explicit, the offer goes unfulfilled. Not because they don't want to help but because they don't know what they can do to help. It is your job as the patient to guide those who truly want to help you.

I also learned not to take it personally when some friends or family couldn't handle my condition. That's their issue and they need to come to grips with that. On the other hand, you learn from that whom you can count on when you need help. Because there are days when you really need a hand, when you need someone to talk to or just be there to listen to you. Your family has to go about its daily routine, as the kids need to get up in the morning, get to school, get home from school, do homework, eat dinner and get ready for bed. So, finding those substitutes is very important.

CHAPTER FOURTEEN

Round Two of Biochemotherapy (Thanksgiving 2005)

My brother David asked how he could help and I asked him to visit during this second round in the hospital. He flew in from New York the day before Thanksgiving and spent the holiday with my family. Friday morning, we drove up to the hospital in Santa Monica and after getting checked in my wife drove back to San Diego. David stayed with my parents during this visit and drove one of their cars. Family came through again.

The first day went smoothly and David left sometime in the early evening. Day two wasn't much different. Day three things changed a little. I wondered whether all of this chemotherapy would cause my hair to fall out and if so, when. Hair loss was one of the more common side effects of most chemotherapies of which we are aware and certainly the one which typically causes us to be most self-conscious. I suspected, and Suzie expected, others to begin to see me in a different light once I lost my hair. Day three is when this process began for me, a little subtle at first, and more thoroughly as the day wore on. It started when I reached up to my head and a small clump of hair fell to the ground. Pulling hair out of your head is kind of like Lays Potato Chips, where nobody eats just one. I reached up again, and more came out. As the morning wore on, I began to lose more hair. By the time David arrived, the hair loss was quite apparent and made him uncomfortable. It took him a couple of days, but he did get over it. Over the course of the next two days, pretty much all my hair had fallen out and I shaved the remaining hair when I got home.

Night three was another milestone event for me. This was probably the first time in all of my cancer history that I became depressed and began to question my survival. I was really down in the dumps and feeling the weight of all this treatment. The hair loss may have triggered these thoughts, although I can't say that for sure. But the cumulative effects were starting to get to me. I also had to listen to the sounds of a patient a few rooms down the hall crying out in pain for hours on end. For the life of me I didn't know why the nurses didn't shut the door to her room, but I remember cringing and hating that sound.

What I remember most about that night though, is not those feelings, but my nurse who came to check on me at about 2:00 a.m. and, seeing how I was feeling, sat with me for almost two hours straight, just talking and listening. He instinctively knew exactly what I needed, which was astonishing. The depth of his compassion was immeasurable. I guess this was another reason a biochemotherapy nurse could only handle two patients – this constant need for attention, even if not for purely medical needs. I feel badly to this day that I don't remember his name. But if I happened to be walking through the hospital corridors and saw him, I would walk right up and give him the most grateful, long, embracing hug in the world. What he did for me that night brought my spirits and confidence back up to normal levels. I love him immensely for that two-hour talk and hope that one day I can tell him to his face.

I was especially grateful for David coming to Los Angeles during round two. His constant presence (except when he left to get his favorite meals, and often brought them back to the hospital just to torment his little brother) was comforting and loving. I really needed that and appreciated that. Days four and five continued the same as round one, except this time I didn't have any problems with my albumin, so my wife was able to get me out of the hospital on day five. We spent the night at the Ambrose Hotel and were back at The Angeles Clinic for the IV infusion on Wednesday.

The biochemotherapy regimen was brutal and took a huge toll on my body. Thankfully I started in pretty strong physical shape. Dr. O'Day said that most patients couldn't even tolerate two rounds. But the protocol was for me to get CT scans and an MRI around day 17 of the cycle to see if the biochemotherapy had any effect on my tumors. The good news was that the scans showed the tumors had shrunk by about 50%. The bad news was Dr. O'Day said I was strong enough to try two more rounds which would begin the next week (remember, those were 21-day cycles).

LESSONS LEARNED

> • *It's okay to be vulnerable and share your emotions*

Night three really taught me that it's okay to show and share your emotions. I don't think I really hid my emotions before that. I genuinely believed I was always going to survive and beat cancer. There was never a doubt in mind. Doubt finally did creep in and it's okay to feel that way. It is virtually impossible to be upbeat all the time and think you're invincible[5]. Being vulnerable is hard, but powerful. My sharing opened me to the love of a nurse whose comforting talk made a huge difference in my well-being.

---

[5] If you're looking for a book about the benefits of having a positive attitude, I highly recommend *Positivity* by Barbara Frederickson.

CHAPTER FIFTEEN

Rounds Three and Four of Biochemotherapy (December 2005/January 2006)

Round three began the same as rounds one and two. I got settled in, then began the IV drip with the sleep-inducing Benadryl, then the three chemotherapies in succession. IL-2 and rigors, hot blankets galore, Tylenol, then the all-time favorite interferon followed. Push slowly, push very slowly I reminded my nurse. Then the oh so lovely uncontrollable diarrhea. What a picture.

Day three brought a really interesting experience for me. Sometime mid-day while watching TV I found myself inside of the TV. In the show I was watching. I don't remember what I was watching but I felt that I was actually inside the TV. This hallucination was incredibly vivid and lifelike. I'd never hallucinated before and this threw me for a loop. As I recall, the hallucination lasted at least an hour. It was a strange sensation indeed to believe I was inside the TV and there was no one there to witness it.

As this was round three and it seemed like I was in for a really tough haul, more extended family started to visit. This was when I began to understand that sometimes people visited me more to make themselves feel better than to make me feel better. My brother Jon wanted to visit and bring his 11-year old son. I asked Jon not to bring his son because I didn't want my nephew to see me in a hospital bed, bloated and lobster red, with three tubes hanging from a rail running into my chest. I didn't think it appropriate and didn't want him to have that memory of me. I was convinced this was not my death bed, so I insisted that he not bring my nephew. What did he do? He brought my nephew, of course. I really didn't understand that behavior. I didn't get why visitors would put their needs or feelings above mine when I was the patient. Unfortunately, I found out from other cancer patients that they experienced interactions like mine as well. I just got used to people not knowing how to deal with my situation and not knowing what to say. That was an all too common experience.

In between round three and four I was doing my best recovery act. The cumulative effect of biochemotherapy was wearing on me. I had experienced significant weight loss, lost all my hair, and my energy level was significantly diminished. I was still eating primarily mint-chip ice cream shakes after four days of IV-infusion at home and still walking multiple times daily. It was all just becoming a greater strain. On one of my walks with my neighbor Jennifer, she recommended I talk with a psychotherapist and referred me to Ellie Werner, a woman to whom I became eternally grateful.

I made an appointment with Ellie and found her spirituality extremely comforting. She "got" me and guided me into a better state of mind. The toll of biochemotherapy was starting to eat at my confidence and Ellie brought me back. Ellie became a wonderful advocate and therapist for me over the years and I was grateful for her encouragement and support. She recommended that I ask my oncologist to write a prescription for Lexapro, an anti-depressant. She also suggested Ambien to help me sleep better and more soundly at night.

Round four of biochemotherapy brought a new surprise and twist. Night three I decided to get up and walk to the bathroom myself instead of ringing for the nurse and waiting for help. I figured no problem, I could do this. This was a big, big, big mistake, although beneficial in the long run. I made it to the toilet alright, but when I tried to get up, I got dizzy and collapsed on the floor. I probably passed out for just a few seconds but managed to call for the nurse who helped me back to my bed.

I shared this experience with Dr. O'Day the next morning during his rounds and he ordered an MRI immediately. Unfortunately, the MRI machine at the hospital was located in a building across the street. Orderlies rolled my hospital bed across the street and up the ramp to the small outbuilding for an MRI. It turned out that I had developed a blood clot in the superior vena cava, the main artery into which the portacath connected. This probably also explained why nurses were having a harder time drawing blood through the portacath. The Coumadin (blood thinner) that I was taking daily to prevent such a clot didn't work.

While this blood clot didn't impact the rest of round four, which ended on day five as planned, the upshot was that I now needed a different blood thinner. Coumadin was a tiny pill and easy to swallow. I graduated to Lovenox, a new prescription, that required a twice-daily injection into my abdomen. At this point, I'd dropped from 165 pounds to 130, and my waist size had gone from a tight 32 to a loose 29. I hadn't seen that waist size since high school. My next problem didn't seem obvious to me but probably should have. With no fat left to pinch, it was difficult to find spots into which to inject the Lovenox. Worse for me was that my wife was uncomfortable giving me injections and refused to help. I think the two months of hooking up IVs into my chest twice a day was just too much for her. I had to learn how to inject myself, which wasn't easy. I couldn't inject myself like nurses did, quickly with no pain. It was much harder for me. I would try and find a new spot, pinch what I could, slowly push the needle in and then gently press down on the syringe. I did this twice daily, and it never got easier.

At the end of this fourth 21-day cycle I went in for more CT scans and an MRI to determine whether the tumors had shrunk any further. Unfortunately, the tumors exhibited no change. The good news was that they hadn't grown any more either. Dr. O'Day explained that the data showed the same survival and recurrence statistics from patients who only had biochemotherapy and those patients that required surgery after biochemotherapy. After a few more weeks of recovery, we scheduled surgeries number five, six and seven.

LESSONS LEARNED

> - *Don't be ashamed about needing a therapist or someone else to whom you can vent*
> - *It's okay to need anti-depressants and sleeping pills*
> - *You are capable of much more than you think*

Don't be ashamed about needing someone to talk to outside of your normal family and friends. We often need a different release and the freedom to share things that we just don't want to share with family. Starting sessions with my therapist was the smartest thing I did during this period. Also, don't be ashamed to ask for sleeping pills or anti-depressants. They are wonderful drugs that help you cope better and build your strength. Your body needs restful sleep as you recover from chemotherapy and sleeping pills can get you there even if your mind wanders to other bad places and thoughts as you're trying to sleep.

I also learned that I was capable of much more than I thought. When faced with adversity, I just needed to power through and do what I needed to do to survive. Self-injections are not a pleasant experience, but I had to do it twice a day. There was no choice. Your challenges could be entirely different. But know in your heart that you are stronger than you think, even when beaten up by chemotherapy or other drugs and surgeries. Armed with that knowledge, you can accomplish what you need, especially when your survival depends on it.

CHAPTER SIXTEEN

A Quick Digression About Finding my Calling Before Surgery Again

I grew up in a traditional Jewish household where charity was an obligation, not a choice. I wrote checks to various charities beginning when I first had savings of my own after my bar mitzvah (13 years old). I always felt good about giving "tzedakah." Once I became an adult and began making a living, my charitable giving increased with income but also became more focused on charities in which I felt a connection beyond the obvious Jewish one. I began giving to the JWCI after my initial diagnosis and gradually directed more of my giving to cancer research.

Something changed in 2004. Suzie and I watched an episode of *HBO's Real Sports with Bryant Gumble* in which Frank Deford, the most prolific sportswriter of our generation, updated a 2001 segment about the Miracle League. Mr. Deford called it one of the most moving pieces he had ever filmed, and Bryant Gumble admitted that he cried when watching it. Anyone else I spoke to who saw the episode remembered it as well, because they cried like we did. In the episode, we were introduced to Lauren Gunder, a 13-year old girl with brittle bone disease who was legally blind. Lauren was a player in the Miracle League, a baseball league for children with mental and/or physical challenges, that was started in Conyers, Georgia. Deford asked Lauren why Miracle League was so important to her. She answered, and I'm paraphrasing somewhat here: "First, I get to live my dream of baseball. Second, I make friends on the field. Third, when I'm on the field, I don't have a disability." How could you not fall in love with this precious attitude?

We were also introduced to Nicholas Slade, a boy who had been born without eyes who played in the Miracle League and sang a memorable version of "Take Me Out to the Ballgame" with Mr. Deford. After watching this episode, we decided to make a donation to the Miracle League. In early 2005, HBO aired a repeat of this episode and this time, we decided that we needed to have a Miracle League in San Diego. The next day we sent a $500 check to the Miracle League and in return received a 3-inch binder with directions for how to start a Miracle League of our own.

As it turned out, many other people across America decided the same thing after watching the original and updated episodes and thus over a hundred Miracle Leagues were formed. Many of those who started Miracle Leagues did not have children with special needs, but, like us, felt compelled to create this opportunity. At this time, I happened to be undergoing major health issues and I worked for one of the kindest bosses in the world, and one of my truly best friends to this day, who let me prioritize getting healthy over working. I was the fourth highest ranking executive in a large company and all he said during this period was "get healthy." I was putting in far fewer hours than full-time work, yet the company paid me a full-time salary and benefits and looked after me in more ways than I can count.

I also have a law background, so I assisted my wife and started the paperwork to form the Miracle League of San Diego and receive non-profit status from the Internal Revenue Service. Creating the Miracle League of San Diego gave me tremendous purpose and something else to work on while recovering. Upon receiving tax-exempt status in June 2005, we built a website so we could begin to attract donations to build our field (the Miracle League requires a rubberized surface to accommodate wheelchairs and the sight impaired). By a very fortunate coincidence, the very day that we launched our website in August, we received a call from Jason Hemmens at the San Diego County Department of Parks and Recreation. Jason had watched the same episode of *Real Sports* and the department wanted to build a Miracle League field at a County park. He approached the national Miracle League office who told him that we had started a Miracle League of San Diego and suggested he call us to partner on the field. We met with Jason and senior staff the next week and began planning our partnership.

Over the next six months I worked with County staff in identifying the best site and preliminary planning. At the end of the day, they chose San Dieguito Park, a location within five miles of our home. This regional park was one of the County's most visited and featured vast open space and ample parking. The reason the County chose this location is because there was already a dilapidated dirt baseball field on the site and by choosing to improve an existing use, we wouldn't face any zoning challenges. The only drawback was that because of the park's location bordering one of San Diego's most expensive neighborhoods, there would not be the opportunity to put lights at the field and operate in the evening.

Once the Parks and Recreation Department selected the site, they then needed to allocate the funds to build the field. In December 2015, we appeared before the County Board of Supervisors supporting the department's request for funding. When funding was approved that night, we knew we were in business.

Let's review the timeline of Miracle League events as they transpired over my 2005 medical calendar. I began all of the IRS paperwork shortly after my first recurrence and recovery from that surgery, followed by the time in Los Angeles for radiation treatment. Building the website and establishing the framework for our organization occurred while I was traveling by train to USC for the multi-peptide vaccine trial. And working with the County Parks and Recreation staff to identify and review sites and ultimately prepare for a presentation to the Board of Supervisors transpired while I was undergoing biochemotherapy. In fact, the Board of Supervisors hearing was shortly after I got home from the hospital for round three. I remember how weak and frail I seemed at the time and the effort it took to speak for two minutes during public comments. But I also remember how powerful, energizing and wonderful it felt when the Board voted unanimously to approve the plans.

I was recently reminded by a friend who was trying to introduce me to potential political advocates at the time, that my instructions to him were that I only had three days open every three weeks in which to meet. Looking back, I can't imagine putting that kind of time constraint on someone trying to help.

But with my biochemotherapy regimen, that was all I could handle.

It's a little difficult to convey the mixed emotions I had throughout 2005. Up to that year, I'd never really felt that cancer affected my daily living. I was upset about the diagnoses, of course, but I always dealt with outcomes quickly and moved on with my work, exercise and living routines. After surgeries I took only a few days to recover. I always weaned myself from pain medications within two days. During the trials at the JWCI and USC, it was just a day trip with no appreciable side effects. But with the radiation therapy and the time I had to miss, and then the biochemotherapy, it was the first time in my life that I couldn't work. And that's a feeling I never wanted to replicate. I liked working. I liked keeping busy. I liked challenges. Not being able to do any of the above was very sobering and humbling for me. To have the Miracle League as something to look forward to that didn't relate to health or compensation was significant. Although I always worked well under pressure, it was a blessing that I could work at my own pace without time deadlines or urgencies, because my body needed rest. The Miracle League filled a terrible void and provided me with inspiration.

Shortly after round four and before the next surgeries (that's for the next chapter), Jason and his staff began the process of requesting proposals from landscape design firms to draft the plans for the project and develop a budget. County regulations required all of the RFP process ("request for proposals") and bidding process to be open to the public at large, which also extended the time frames for taking action. It took about two months from the time the RFP was posted on the County's website until staff selected the winning bidder with some input from us. The preliminary budget left a substantial gap to be raised by the Miracle League of San Diego, and by extension, from me and my wife. But because of the way County funding worked, if we weren't able to raise the funds by the end of 2006, the allocation from County funds would revert back to general use for the calendar year 2007. Armed with these deadlines, we began to think about how to raise that money before we focused on actual operations.

LESSONS LEARNED

> • *You never know where you will find your passion but when you do, pursue it vigorously*

I still don't know how individuals find their passion. What I do know is that when you do discover your passion, it will likely surprise you. While I grew up enjoying baseball and going to games, I was never what you would call a huge baseball fan. But something in the HBO episode touched me at a time when I needed to find other meaning. I didn't have full strength to work at my paying job and my travel for the company decreased significantly. My boss encouraged me to focus on my recovery, but I just couldn't sit still. Instead, I dove headfirst into forming the Miracle League and all that entailed. For the first time in my life, I wasn't just writing checks to a charity, but I was devoting significant time to our mission.

All charitable organizations need both donors and workers. I'd always been a donor. But I found that working at establishing the Miracle League, developing the relationship with the County, forming the partnership and presenting to the Board of Supervisors, gave me enormous and much needed purpose.

CHAPTER SEVENTEEN

Surgeries Number Five, Six, Seven and Eight (January/February 2006)

Let's bring this story back to reality and my next surgeries. As I've said before, when I needed surgery I scheduled the first available appointment when I could be Dr. Essner's first patient. Unfortunately, the blood clot I developed during biochemotherapy slowed down my process. The presence of blood thinners posed a tremendous risk to me during surgery. I therefore had to wait five days for the blood thinner Lovenox to exit my system.

Back to Los Angeles we went with our now usual room at the Ambrose Hotel. We of course ate our favorite sushi for dinner to put me in the best possible spirits. Routine became very important for me. The next morning, we showed up about an hour before surgery to get checked in and go through the prep. Then came my longest surgery to date. Why? And why was I counting this as three surgeries?

Surgery five was the right lymphadenectomy on the same line as surgery three (I received a JP drain again). Surgery six was a right axella dissection to remove all lymph nodes under my right armpit. Surgery seven was to remove the subcutaneous tumor on my chest. Oh, and just for good measure and not counting, Dr. Essner had to remove the portacath from my chest. That was a lot of work and perfectly understandable why I insisted on being Dr. Essner's first patient. Moreover, the lymphadenectomies had become progressively more difficult as my neck had accumulated significant scar tissue from the prior operations. Hence, it required more patience and more work to cut through the scar tissue and remove the remaining lymph nodes and tumors.

I spent another lonely night in the hospital and waited for morning to come. Morning meant Dr. Essner checking on me and releasing me to go home. This time, however, the assistant surgeon arrived first. Naturally, my first question to her was "when I can go home?" To my surprise, she suggested that I spend another night in the hospital because I had just had two major surgeries (neither removing the tumor on the chest nor removing the portacath were considered major) and insurance would cover another night. I told her that I wanted to go home. She kept pushing but I guess that as an assistant surgeon, she didn't have enough experience with patients like me who recovered quickly AND understood that leaving the hospital quickly was the best medicine. In my mind, only bad things happened in hospitals. Thankfully I prevailed because I was able to pass the two tests required to be released – I could pee freely and I could hold down solid food. I'd like to think that having the anesthesiologist repeat my healing statements (thanks again to Scott and my favorite book) that included I would pee freely and I would eat mint ice cream helped me in this aspect.

One of the things I hated most about surgeries was the inability to drive myself for a prolonged period of time. This time, because of the extensive work on the right side (neck and armpit dissections) and significantly less range of motion, this period seemed longer. It was extremely difficult to back up a car and look over my shoulder. This of course put a greater strain on home life because I required my wife to drive me everywhere. If she couldn't, I needed to find other rides. And when I desperately wanted to have lunch out with friends, they needed to pick me up at the house. That became a burden on my friends who were taking off from work to keep me company and bring the outside world into my life.

Another thing I hated about having surgery two hours away from home was the requirement to drive back to Los Angeles to have Dr. Essner examine me and remove the stitches when ready. The JP drains also needed to be removed and that couldn't be done locally. But, I had made the important choice to have one of the finest surgical oncologists in America be my surgeon and I did what was necessary to ensure the best care possible. If that meant extra travel, so be it.

What made matters worse for my family and me was that just three weeks after surgeries five, six and seven, I needed surgery number eight. This time, Dr. Essner performed a lymphadenectomy on the left side of my neck. This surgery was three weeks later because it was not advisable to operate on both sides of my neck at the same time as recovery would have been extremely brutal. So up to Los Angeles we went, back to the Ambrose, back to Sushi Sasabune, and back to St. John's Hospital at 7:00 a.m. Again, a long surgery followed with another JP drain and another night in the hospital. As per my

personal protocol, I left the hospital as early as possible the following day.

As one can image, the range of motion in my neck was now
even worse, thereby prolonging my absence from driving. But
I powered through the recovery as always and found my way
back to Los Angeles about ten days later to remove the JP drain
and the stitches. At this point I had virtually identical hockey
stick scars on both sides of my neck. But Dr. Essner's stitching
was as precise and clean as that of a plastic surgeon or better,
so the scars were not particularly noticeable unless one looked
closely or was told about the surgeries.

My mindset then was hopeful that Dr. Essner had removed
all last vestiges of cancer from my body. According to Dr.
O'Day, the evidence was that the combination of surgery and
biochemotherapy was just as effective as biochemotherapy
alone in prolonging survival. I was confident as always that I
was on the right path.

LESSONS LEARNED

> • ***Don't forget to manage travel and driving is-
> sues – the stress on families can become
> overwhelming***

I mention all the travel and driving issues because they are
significant while dealing with illness. I was fortunate to have
great doctors, they just weren't local. I believe you need to find
the best doctor in your particular specialty and if travel is required you need to find the means to do so. I understand that
financial constraints were not a concern to me as they would be
to the vast majority of patients. Nonetheless, if you are faced

with a medical battle that requires travel to get the best possible care, I would encourage you to explore every means available to you. There are probably local-based non-profit organizations near you that provide assistance to cancer patients specifically for these purposes.

However, you must recognize that travel and transportation issues really take a toll on your family and caregivers. As patients, we tend to think selfishly and place our needs first to ensure fast recoveries. That's okay, we have every right and need to be selfish. If there is ever any time that selfishness is appropriate it's when you are in the midst of health battles. On the other hand, we need to be cognizant of how our situation impacts others. To the extent you can identify those friends and family who can help take the strain and burdens off of your immediate caregivers, you should. Take advantage of those friendships and ask for exactly what you need.

A quick note about driving and rides from friends. When I was making these trips, ride-share services like Uber and Lyft did not exist. I imagine that if Uber or Lyft were around in 2005 and 2006, I would have been one of their most frequent customers. I'm sure there are other advancements in services and technology that would have benefited me during my journey and that will benefit others during theirs today and in the future.

CHAPTER EIGHTEEN

Clinical Trial Number Four (February 2006)

Shortly after surgery number eight, Dr. O'Day wanted me to start another clinical trial to prevent recurrence. In his experience, a maintenance trial of high-dose IL-2 and Granulocyte-macrophage colony-stimulating factor ("GM-CSF) could be beneficial post bio-chemotherapy and surgery. I had received IL-2 as one of the two immunotherapies included in the biochemotherapy and GM-CSF was another immunotherapy. Together these drugs were believed to stimulate my immune system to fight off cancer.

So, what did this trial entail? Yet another two days in a hospital to deliver the high-dose IL-2 followed by self-injections of the GM-CSF. I wasn't anxious to head to Los Angeles again, especially for just two nights in the hospital. That protocol would put a bigger strain on my family. I asked Dr. O'Day if a local oncologist could administer the high-dose IL-2 in a San Diego hospital. He was skeptical at first but encouraged me to find a San Diego oncologist with the requisite experience. As it happened, my father-in-law was battling prostate cancer and he had a San Diego oncologist with whom I met to discuss the protocol. After several back and forth conversations between Dr. O'Day and Dr. James Sinclair in San Diego, Dr. O'Day approved of Dr. Sinclair administering the high-dose IL-2.

For the first time in seven years I was admitted to a local hospital, a place where I had no prior history. This was a little weird for me as I was so accustomed to the procedures and locations at St. John's in Santa Monica. Thankfully I also had a close friend and gastroenterologist in San Diego, who saw patients in the same hospital. He came to my room as soon as I was admitted and provided me a lot of comfort. Unfortunately, what happened next was one of my worst experiences to date. For years I'd been having IVs placed in my arm or hand or wrist. I had good veins and never did a nurse need to stick me more than once to find a good vein. I was what the nurses called an "easy stick." For whatever reason I couldn't explain, the nurse assigned to me stuck me three times and still couldn't find a vein. I can't explain how frustrating that was as I'd never experienced that small pain before. It really made me empathetic for those patients who were "hard sticks." Now here is where my experience as a patient came into play. After three attempts, I insisted on bringing in a more experienced nurse, who of course found a good vein on the first try. In hindsight, I'm amazed that I gave the first nurse three tries and didn't ask for a new nurse after two attempts.

Now that I had a good IV inserted, the nurse began the high-dose IL-2. I knew to expect the rigors, so I asked the nurse to have warm blankets handy. What was interesting to me is that the nurse wasn't aware that the rigors were a standard side effect. This was when I began to understand the difference between being in a hospital with nurses and doctors who have significant experience in a particular treatment or protocol and being in a hospital with nurses and doctors who were following a protocol that was new to them. Although the instructions were quite detailed and clear, these nurses just didn't have the depth of knowledge that my St. John's nurses had.

The next day Dr. Sinclair's partner visited my room and conducted a basic exam. Much to my dismay, as he felt around my neck (checking glands and lymph nodes), he seemed to be spending a lot of time feeling around the left side. He was concerned about some swelling and thought I might have lymphatic disease again. He decided that since I'd already begun the high-dose IL-2 treatment, we should continue the protocol and I should follow up with Dr. O'Day once released. I was astonished and fearful that not even a month after surgery number eight, my first lymphadenectomy on the left side of my neck, I might have more tumors in the same spot. Nonetheless we continued the treatment and I was released the following day.

Now that the high-dose IL-2 was completed, I began self-administering GM-CSF. Because of the blood clot we found during round four of biochemotherapy, I was still injecting myself daily with Lovenox. The GM-CSF doubled my burden. In addition to injecting myself twice in my super-skinny, no-fat belly (I struggled to find different spots around my belly to pinch), I had to fill the syringe. I was quite impressed with how I'd learned some basic nursing skills, not that I ever really wanted to learn them. But I managed and continued with my four weeks of the injections.

This was a month where I really needed but didn't get more involvement from my wife. It would have been so much easier for me if she had taken the responsibility to fill the syringes and to give me the injections. I asked for her help, but she refused. If she had said it was too difficult I might have understood. Instead, I got a mumbled response that "if you wanted a better caregiver you should have married someone else." Comments like that were extremely hurtful, unhelpful and set the tone for the eventual decline and end of our marriage.

During these four weeks at home, I had Miracle League activities to keep my mind occupied. In February, I attended a hearing at a regional planning commission that had funds available for projects in San Dieguito Park. County Parks and Recreation staff had presented a grant request that, if approved, would have substantially reduced the Miracle League's financial obligation and would have accelerated our development timeline. I arrived on a cold evening when I had to don many layers of clothing to keep me warm. I was tired and thin and did not have as strong a voice as usual. But I spoke passionately for my two minutes of allotted time and fielded questions from board members who seemed inclined to approve the grant. Then I learned my first lesson about local politics – even though you might have a wonderful proposal that fits squarely within a commission's objectives, and even though a majority of those on the panel seemed to be in favor of your proposal, you might not win. It seemed that the chair of the commission had an entirely different agenda on his mind and had deep-seated resentment for Parks and Recreation Staff. Apparently, he felt that staff had neglected one of his favorite projects over a year ago and he raised questions based solely on his priorities. Because the Miracle League field was not his priority, he essentially sabotaged our proposal and ensured a no vote on the grant request. What frustrated me most was that he didn't even care about the merits of our project. He only cared about his own agenda. That's local politics in a nutshell.

About this time, we also asked the San Diego Padres to partner with us or make a substantial donation to help develop our Miracle League field. The Padres had a program called Little Padres Parks with a mission to redevelop 35 baseball fields around the county over the course of seven years. We were fortunate that the Padres elected to designate our field a Little Padres Park and to devote resources to our process.

Let's get back to the health journey. After 28 days of GM-CSF, I went back to The Angeles Clinic for scans and a check-up. Unfortunately, Dr. Sinclair's partner was correct, and I had more tumors in the left side of my neck. It was time to call Dr. Essner to schedule surgery number nine, which I scheduled as quickly as possible.

LESSONS LEARNED

> - *Remember that even in a hospital setting you need to be your own best advocate*
> - *Make sure your doctors and nurses have significant experience administering your health protocol*

My time in this hospital taught me again how important it is for you to be your own advocate. I knew my body. I knew I was an easy stick. And when that nurse couldn't find a good vein, I spoke up and insisted on a new nurse. If you haven't been through as many procedures as I had, you might consider this the norm and not have pushed as quickly for a different nurse. But you have to speak up for yourself as soon as something doesn't seem right. Don't wait for someone else to speak up for you because they won't or can't. Only you know your body and all your experiences so be confident in asking for what you need. Ask questions when you're not sure. Don't be passive about your care.

I also learned how important it is to be treated by physicians and nurses with extensive experience in your particular disease or with a particular protocol. It became more frustrating than it should have to undergo treatment in San Diego instead of Los Angeles. We made the choice to have the IL-2 treatment in San Diego because it was only two nights in the hospital but in hindsight, I wouldn't have made that same choice.

CHAPTER NINETEEN

Surgery Number Nine (March 2006)

I've mentioned ad nauseum how my routine became so important to me. So, as you can guess, I went back to Santa Monica, back to the Hotel Ambrose, back to Sushi Sasabune and back to St. John's Hospital at 7:00 a.m. And I guess I became a little routine for Dr. Essner as well. He operated at 8:00 a.m. (or really within an hour of the set time), checked on me at night, checked on me again in the morning and released me. This time Dr. Essner cut a second hockey stick along the left side of my neck below the first one from surgery number eight. So now I had matching double hockey stick scars, though as I mentioned before, neither were very noticeable. I also had a JP drain again. How crazy is it that my ninth surgery could be described in just one paragraph?

The only thing non-routine about surgery nine was the JP drain that wouldn't stop draining. Typically, the drain was empty within five days and would be removed. Removal was very simple, but also a little weird. The JP drainage bulb was connected to a very tiny tube that terminated inside my neck through a very small slit. The end that was inside the neck had little burrs that enabled it to stay in the proper place. Removing the drain was an awkward feeling as the furry end was pulled through such a small opening that didn't even require a stitch to close.

The problem was this drain kept filling and didn't seem to stop. And it leaked a little at the point it entered my skin. My friend Scott's wife Zoe, who was a nurse, became my new best friend as it related to the JP drain. Zoe let me stop by her house or office every few days to examine the drain and the site. Finally, after about two weeks, I was able to return to Dr. Essner's office to remove the drain and stitches.

After nine surgeries and four clinical trials, I finally began to question whether I would really beat stage four melanoma, especially given the fact that surgery nine was about a month after surgery eight, and in the exact same location. These feelings of helplessness became very pervasive. My thoughts began to waver between how I would feel if I couldn't see my children Sam and Jordan grow up and, worse still, how would they feel without my being there? Once those thoughts entered my consciousness, this cycle continued virtually unabated. And because my relationship with my wife was strained, it was difficult for me to share with her the depth of my concerns. Instead, I began to share these feelings and this burden I felt with my closest friends. Each was an empathetic listener who gave me all the time I needed to vent. Their friendship and support went way above the call of duty.

Armed with a new sense of uncertainty, I decided it was time to do some things with my family that we might not be able to do again. What kinds of things? Bucket list items. Fun travel. The first trip was to Las Vegas to see the Elton John Red

Piano show at Caesars Palace. My old boss Andy got us four 2nd row center seats. Another business colleague arranged a complimentary suite at the luxurious Venetian Hotel. The entire weekend was incredible from start to finish.

A little later we traveled to Kauai, Hawaii for a week. The hotel we chose had an amazing pool slide that seemed to stretch for miles. I remember Sam, Jordan and I walking to the top of the slide, waiting our turn, sliding down, then back up again, for what seemed like hours on end. I spent many a nap time in my favorite spot – a hammock by the ocean. We went through quite a few bottles of sunscreen that week.

Meanwhile, I noticed a couple of small lumps growing on my back. I didn't share this with the family because I didn't want to scare anyone. I knew that I would be exploring new clinical trial options when I returned so I kept the feelings to myself, which was difficult to do. But I felt this was the right approach for my family.

What was weird about the tumors on my back was that this was only the second time in my melanoma history that I could actually feel a tumor. All of the other times the tumors were in lymph nodes or soft tissue, hidden from touch.

We also ran into friends from San Diego who were staying at the same hotel. The father was a medical researcher with some melanoma experience. We spoke at length in the pool about my latest history and prospects for other clinical trials. He argued with me that I could get better care in San Diego with an oncologist who specialized in melanoma. I had met this oncologist before, and although I found him very kind and likeable, he did not offer the breadth or depth of clinical trials that were offered at the JWCI and The Angeles Clinic. I guess it must have felt very obnoxious to my friend, a medical researcher, for me to tell him that I knew more about the prospective treatments than he did. But given how long I had been battling on a daily basis, I was very confident and comfortable in my opinions. And I knew that I was being treated by the top medical oncologists on the West Coast. When it comes to clinical trials, I believed it a must to find a center with the broadest experience possible as only in such a center would I find the very best option.

When we returned home, I also called two friends with whom I had worked beginning in 1985, Chris McGovern and Scott Schumann. They had kept up with my battles and I knew that I really wanted to see them. Chris lived in Connecticut and Scott lived in Cleveland. We therefore planned a trip in April to Chicago (somewhat midway between the three of us) where we could just hang out for a few days, catch a Cubs game at Wrigley Field, eat some good food and watch some great live music. We all bought tickets and the trip was settled.

LESSONS LEARNED

> • **Spend quality time with loved ones while you can or even just think you can**

The key lesson during this time period was that once I actually felt the possibility that I wouldn't survive, I took concrete actions to spend time with my family doing things we might never do again. I'm thankful of course that these weren't the last times we traveled together and saw concerts and such. But nonetheless, when faced with that prospect, I'd encourage you to act. Be bold. Go places. Share your love with family and friends. Reacquaint yourself with old friends. Do whatever makes you happy while still fighting for your life. Never give up the fight. Because you never know if you'll win.

As I think more about this lesson, and I've done so many, many times, I realize that we don't need a cancer or chronic disease diagnosis to choose this path. For me, though, it took nine surgeries and four clinical trials to realize that I had a choice to make about how to live the rest of my life, no matter how long that might be. I often feel sad when I realize I could have reprioritized my life long before melanoma took control.

CHAPTER TWENTY

Clinical Trial Number Five (April 2006)

When I came home from Hawaii, I visited Dr. O'Day to get new scans and discuss clinical trial options. I remember this visit for many reasons, aside from the fact that it took virtually all day. Now that I was being treated at The Angeles Clinic and not in the hospital setting or the JWCI, I had the opportunity to have my scans taken in the same office as the doctor's office and treatment facility. I was able to get an appointment for a CT scan first thing in the morning and have the results within a couple of hours. After the scan I was starving (one can't eat for eight hours before a CT scan), so I walked across the street to a diner and relaxed as best I could, knowing that I had at least two tumors on my back.

When I finally saw Dr. O'Day, he discussed two options. The first was a trial combining CarboTaxol (actually Carbo-Taxol was a combination of two chemotherapy drugs – Carboplatin and Paclitaxel) and Sorafenib. CarboTaxol was chemotherapy administered intravenously every three weeks and Sorafenib was a pill taken daily. CarboTaxol was typically used to treat small cell lung cancer and ovarian cancer. Soraf-enib was a targeted therapy that was approved to treat kidney cancer and was thought to work on melanomas that exhibited the B-raf mutation (Sorafenib was thus a B-raf inhibitor). This time period in cancer research was around the beginning of targeted therapies and B-raf was a promising approach. At that time, however, there wasn't a reliable biomarker[6] that would indicate whether my tumors had the B-raf mutation. A requirement to enter the trial was that I had a solid tumor of at least 10 centimeters in size.

The second option was a new drug called Ipilimumab being developed by a drug company called Medarex. Ipilimumab, or "Ipi" for short, was also called anti-CTLA4 antibody because of the way it worked. Also administered intravenously, Ipilimumab was a monoclonal antibody that activated the immune system by targeting CTLA-4 (cytotoxic T-lymphocyte-associated protein 4), a protein receptor that downregulated the immune system. Dr. O'Day was one of the first oncologists in the country to conduct trials using Ipilimumab. At that time, there was only one clinical trial open to me that had three "arms" with varying levels of the drug (either one, three or ten milligrams per kilogram of body weight). Dr. O'Day knew that a new trial would be opening soon with only one arm at the higher dose of ten milligrams per kilogram of body weight. He also knew that based upon my general health I could tolerate the ten milligrams and wanted me to wait for that trial to open

---

[6] A biomarker would be a measurable indicator of whether one had a specific mutation. The test would need to be a blood test or through a biopsy of a tumor. Biomarkers are very important when considering targeted therapies.

instead of risking my being assigned randomly to one of the arms with a lower dosage.

We therefore chose to begin the CarboTaxol/Sorafenib trial as soon as possible to hopefully shrink or limit the growth of the existing tumors. Which brings the discussion back to tumors, and more importantly, how a radiologist measures the size of said tumors. Dr. O'Day and I walked over to the radiologist's office to look at the scans on his computer. I had multiple tumors but the one on the back was the largest and therefore the one we measured. The radiologist selected two points on the computer screen and drew a line between them. He then measured that line. But where those points were chosen was the important factor. The closer one zoomed in, the more precise the measurement. Moreover, the radiologist had the ability to rotate the view and get different angles. It took my radiologist several different attempts to identify a straight line that measured 10 centimeters. But he ultimately was able to determine the tumor was 10 centimeters and I was therefore qualified to begin the trial.

Another requirement to enter this trial was to have a bone scan to determine whether the cancer had spread into my bones. Thankfully, The Angeles Clinic also had a bone scan machine and I was able to take that exam while there that day. The results showed that the cancer had not spread to my bones. I thought I was ready to begin the trial immediately.

Not so fast I learned. All of my scans, pathology reports and blood draws needed to be sent to a central lab to be read uniformly by the drug company's contract research organization ("CRO"). Moreover, I required an eye exam prior to and after treatment because one risk factor was blindness. The CRO had to rule out any eye damage prior to my beginning the trial. And, of course I had to read and initial every page of and sign the clinical trial consent form (about 30 pages). We arranged all the details and I headed home and promptly made an appointment with my eye doctor. After completing that exam and sending it off to the CRO, I waited for their approval.

I expected this approval to come within a week and I was very anxious to begin as I did not like the thought of tumors growing. Being the pushy patient that I was, I called the CRO office to check on the progress. That was not a pleasant call and for the first time I could remember, I was actually rude to a medical professional. It seems that although Dr. O'Day's office had sent the scans and blood draws in a timely fashion, and although my eye doctor sent her paperwork in a timely fashion, the CRO's lab had not yet processed my blood work which effectively delayed my treatment for another week. I was livid at this prospect and yelled at the clerk as if the delay was his fault. I'm sure I used profanity as well. I'm not proud of this outburst but a week delay meant my tumors kept growing and I just could not accept that. I had to accept that as there was nothing I nor my oncologists could do. There was no excuse for treating someone the way I did, and I tried very hard to never do that again.

The approval came a few days later and I was able to start the treatment. Unfortunately, the treatment protocol had me in Los Angeles smack dab in the middle of my planned trip to Chicago to meet Scott and Chris, so I had to cancel. That sucked but such is the life of a cancer patient. Up to The Angeles Clinic I drove for the first IV infusion of CarboTaxol. My favorite nurse Cathy was there to meet me and get me settled. Unlike the IV infusions during biochemotherapy when I had a portacath, I now needed an IV line inserted into a vein. Cathy stuck me the first time with no pain whatsoever. I vowed from that day forward to always choose Cathy to stick me if she was in the office. This was probably irrational and maybe a little obnoxious to other nurses as they were just as capable. But I felt right with Cathy and I felt this was my prerogative. I've been told by other nurses that my stubbornness was very common. I lived by the motto that it was okay to be selfish when I was battling disease. As long as I was not negatively impacting procedures and timing, I figured it was fine for me ask for little things that made a difference to me.

As this was a true chemotherapy treatment, I was started on the famous and lovely Benadryl to prevent allergic reactions (and really just knock me out). I couldn't really fall asleep while sitting in these recliners because (1) nurse Cathy or Secela would wake me up every 30 minutes to take vitals (temperature and blood pressure) and (2) there were other patients in the recliners around me, most accompanied by a spouse or other caregiver. Lucky for me I could fall asleep rather quickly and I was able to nap. I left after about three hours with a prescription bottle filled with the Sorafenib.

What about side effects? There were always side effects. One of Sorafenib's noted side effects was peripheral neuropathy, or tingling hands and feet. In my case, the neuropathy came very quickly in the form of pins and needles that felt exactly like when you hit your funny bone. Unfortunately, this could arise almost any time, even from simple acts like flushing the toilet. The pain shot down my arm so strongly that it brought me to tears. I would also get these feelings in my feet and toes. I did not like this side effect at all. Unfortunately, there were no medications to relieve the neuropathy and I suffered through the duration of this trial.

I was given a research report detailing the potential side effects from CarboTaxol which included nausea, low white and red blood cell counts, achiness, etc. I remember the literature said that hair loss would typically begin between days 18 and 23. The reason I remembered this particular detail was that Day 18 found me in Central California (the town of Visalia to be precise) with a member of the San Diego Padres and a member of the development team from the San Diego County Parks and Recreation Department. We were there to observe Miracle League play at the only other Miracle League in California. My hair had grown back by this time and I was feeling pretty good. I was due back in Los Angeles a few days later for the second dosage of CarboTaxol. We had made the six-hour drive to Visalia on day 17 and spent the night in a local motel. Well, the next morning, while standing in the shower, I began to shampoo. Or so I thought. As I began to lather up, I felt a large clump of hair come out into my hands. And then more. This went on for about 15 minutes and most of my hair fell out except for a few weird spots. I remember looking into the bottom of the tub and seeing basically my entire head of hair clogging the drain. I scooped up as much as possible and put it in the trash can. I often wondered what the maid who cleaned the room thought when she went to empty that trash can. The bottom line here was that the literature was 100% accurate as to hair loss beginning on day 18. I remember the looks I received from my travel companions when I met them for breakfast. One day I had a full head of hair, the next day not so much. They were aware of my treatment but certainly didn't expect to see bald Dan Engel. Thankfully, I had a baseball hat to wear the rest of the trip that covered most of my head.

While the three of us on this trip had all watched the same episode of *HBO's Real Sports*, none of us had ever attended a Miracle League game. When we arrived, we met the founders of the Visalia Miracle League, another couple like me and Suzie who did not have children with special needs but were inspired by the same episode. They operated Burger King franchises, so their snack bar was pretty well stocked with equipment from some of their locations. But that just spoke to the physical facility.

The games were something else altogether and we were blown away by the fact that they had an announcer for each of the two games we witnessed. The excitement from the children when they heard their names called was infectious. We sat in awe watching the incredible action and happiness on the field. And we were delighted that the founders shared their time to tell us about their operations, how they held a pizza party the night before opening day to give uniforms, etc. On our drive home we couldn't stop talking about our experience. It was so meaningful to have a representative of the Padres with us because he decided on his own that the Padres needed to donate a sound system and score board to provide the same experience as in Visalia. We hadn't even thought to put anything like that in our budget.

Back to my experience on this clinical trial. The drugs didn't seem to be doing anything at all and I felt another tumor growing on my chest. At the end of the three months total, new scans showed that I had a total of eight tumors. I had three subcutaneous tumors, or tumors just under my skin that I could feel, and five lymphatic tumors, or tumors concentrated in the lymph nodes. The lymphatic tumors were around my neck and heart. The only good news was that Medarex finally was about to open the new clinical trial for Ipilimumab with a single arm receiving 10 milligrams per kilogram of body weight. This study was labeled MDX-08 and I was set to begin in July.

LESSONS LEARNED

> • **Make sure your oncologist has direct access to scans and not just written reports**

The key medical lesson during this time period was how important it is for your oncologist to have direct access to the scans and radiologist reading your scans. In my case, had Dr. O'Day and I not walked into the radiologist's office to view my scans, it's possible that the radiologist would not have tried as many measurement points and that his official report would not have listed the tumor at 10 cm, thereby rendering me ineligible to start the clinical trial.

On a more personal and not medical level, I also started learning about the power of the Miracle League and the effect it had on all of its participants. After witnessing the Visalia games first hand, I couldn't stop thinking about how incredible it would be to bring that opportunity to San Diego. I was energized to push forward with our plans.

CHAPTER TWENTY ONE

I Still Have a Job, Don't I?

With all the treatments I'd endured, I did not have much time or energy to work. I was fortunate my employer was ok with that. As I wrote earlier, my boss was a kind and generous person named Sid, whom in the Yiddish language would be called a "mensch."[7] Once the recurrences started coming, Sid told me to just get healthy and I took him at his word.

But the company, Applied Underwriters, continued to pay me my full salary and health benefits and I felt an obligation to do what I could, which wasn't too terribly much. I could never shake the feeling that I wasn't doing enough for our company. One of my key roles was developing and maintaining our five-year plan and operating budget. Thankfully I had improved the model over many years, so it required relatively little maintenance other than monthly inputs which I was still able to do.

Prior to 2005, I would travel to San Francisco at least two to three times a month for three to four days to work in our

---

[7] A mensch is a someone to admire and emulate, someone of noble character. The key to being "a real mensch" is nothing less than character, rectitude, dignity, a sense of what is right, responsible, decorous. (Rosten, Leo. 1968. The Joys of Yiddish. New York: Pocket Books. 237)

corporate offices with senior staff. I enjoyed the camaraderie that I developed and the late-night discussions about our business and strategy. I would also travel to our back-office operations in Omaha, Nebraska every other month or so. During 2005, those visits were extremely limited, and I really missed the human interactions. I also missed the intellectual stimulation of the work and I suppose my efforts toward the Miracle League filled that void to some extent.

Another key role was to help position the company for sale and to be the primary liaison with our investment bankers during the process. I ran all prospective investor/purchaser meetings in both San Francisco and Omaha. Much of that process occurred initially in 2004 and spilled into early 2005 so I was heavily involved. None of those efforts turned into a transaction. But in early 2006, we began negotiating a sale to a large public company, Berkshire Hathaway. Although I had provided the financial model that was the framework for the negotiations and sale, I was unable to participate in any of those meetings. Ultimately the sale closed in May 2006.

It was emotionally very difficult for me to handle not being involved. I was so used to working and contributing on a high level that not being involved was killing me inside. I talked to Sid as often as I could, but these conversations weren't a substitute for being face-to-face and the interactions were less than fulfilling for me. Once the sale closed, my responsibilities diminished significantly as probably 80% of what I did over the past four years was directly related to improving efficiencies, managing financial performance and metrics, and positioning the company for sale. It was clear to me that I had worked my way out of a job. As we continued on in 2006, Sid and I talked about my future role and he offered me a chance to stay with the company in a different capacity if I were willing to move to either San Francisco or Omaha. I wasn't willing to do that for several reasons, but foremost was that I felt a need to stay near my family and my doctors.

Knowing my job was ending, even though for a good reason, didn't sit well with Suzie. I felt comfortable financially and believed I would find a good job in the near future, so I was happy to bide my time looking. Suzie, on the other hand, felt I had an obligation to support the family at a level to which we were accustomed. She wanted me to search hard for a job as soon as possible, while I wanted to take a breather. This tension between us never quite dissipated.

As I wasn't working much, I was able to devote more time to getting our Miracle League field built. We had a budget gap to fill and needed to raise the money before the County could even find a contractor. This was when my former boss and mentor came to the rescue. I first met Andy Astrachan in the summer of 1985 while I was a summer associate at Salomon Brothers, a major New York-based investment banking firm. When I moved to Los Angeles from New York in 1990, we reconnected and got together infrequently. As I got to know Andy better, I learned that he spent every Friday afternoon in Watts (an impoverished area of Los Angeles) mentoring African-American kids. He helped them with school and life. I met one of his mentees, Johnny, a young man whose mother was in jail for drugs and whom Andy had brought into his home so that he could attend and graduate from a safe high school. Johnny later went to Arizona State to play football, and ultimately went to law school. His application essay was about how Andy changed his life. Andy's life always had purpose, and I admired this deeply, especially when I went to work for him.

Andy was also an investor in Applied Underwriters, the company at which I was working. When we sold the company, Andy, Sid and the other major shareholders received substantial returns on their investment. My proceeds from the small share that I owned enabled me to pursue some of my philanthropic efforts since then.

Andy and I were very close, and in late 2006, I shared with him the story of our Miracle League. Andy was a huge sports fan and he remembered watching the same episode of *HBO's Real Sports*. Andy committed on the spot to write the first $50,000 check and helped me approach all of the other shareholders, who made commitments between $10,000 and $50,000 each. In December 2016, within a month of Andy's involvement, we had raised enough money to donate to the County of San Diego, so they could hire contractors.

LESSONS LEARNED

> • *Live your life with loyalty, integrity and respect*

It's hard to discern lessons learned during this period. But for me it can be summed up in three words: loyalty, integrity and respect. These three words drove how I lived my life both personally and professionally. I was fortunate to work with and surround myself with others who shared the same traits and values. I'd known and worked with Andy for over 20 years. I'd known and worked with Sid for over ten years. And throughout all that time I was devoted and loyal to both, and that loyalty was mutual. I respected them, and they respected me. I always maintained my integrity and insisted on working for others like them who operated with the same integrity. I suppose that is why when I was seeking donors for the Miracle League, Andy and Sid stepped up and helped make it happen.

Another way to describe this lesson is one I teach today in my current non-profit organization. That is, influence is all relational. I built strong relationships over the years through dedicated effort and immense loyalty. I deliberately focused on deepening ties with important colleagues rather than building a network of loose connections. In 2018 terms, my fewer deep connections were much more valuable to me, for example, than having 1,000 Facebook friends. These deep relationships enabled me to exert influence for a good cause, the Miracle League of San Diego.

Another quick digression about integrity (or honesty if you will) and why that is so important to me. My father was a CPA and lawyer who was a noted tax expert. While I was an undergraduate student at UCLA, my father invited me to a lecture he was giving about film finance. I'd never seen him speak publicly so I was excited to attend. I will never forget how he was introduced to the audience. Paraphrasing, it went as follows: "When you're putting together a film, everyone has their hand out. The producer, the director, the actors, the writers, the lawyers, the accountants, everyone is looking for a payday. Over the years, I've tried to give Morrie Engel extra money countless times, but he only takes what he's earned. He is the most honest guy in the business." That stuck with me and is why integrity is job one with me.

CHAPTER TWENTY TWO

Clinical Trial Number Six – Ipilimumab, MDX 08 (July 2006)

When Dr. O'Day explained the Ipilimumab protocol and treatment plan, he said that I should expect to be at The Angeles Clinic for an hour and a half IV infusion given every three weeks for a total of four infusions. After that, I would have scans at three months and again at six months. Also, if at the end of six months I showed no evidence of disease, I would be eligible to receive infusions every three months indefinitely as "maintenance therapy." I remember walking back to Cathy, one of my favorite chemo nurses, to say goodbye for the day and she set me straight in her usual plain-spoken way. She said, "uh uh baby, plan on the whole day." I love Cathy so much for so many reasons, but her love, compassion and sense of humor stand out. She told me that I had to arrive early for blood work, then I had to wait for the lab to complete the analysis, then I had to wait for Dr. O'Day to review the labs and examine me, then I had to wait for Dr. O'Day to call the drug company to approve treatment, then I had to wait for the drug to be delivered from the other office so the nurse could mix the proper amount into the IV solution, then I had to wait for the nurse to do that, then I had to get called back from the reception area to sit in the reclining chair for the hour and a half infusion, then there was an hour observation period to make sure I was okay and didn't have any adverse reactions. That sounded a lot different than "an hour and a half." I needed these details so I could plan my travel accordingly. There are few things more important to a patient than managing expectations. If I had only listened to Dr. O'Day, and not talked to Cathy, I would have been a miserable, angry person after the whole-day affair.

Since I had to be at The Angeles Clinic early in the morning, I spent the night before at my now usual hotel spot, the Hotel Ambrose. Why did I always stay at hotels in Los Angeles even though I had family there? The odd thing for me, and this was difficult for my family to understand as they always offered and truly wanted me to stay with them, was that nights before treatments were introspective, unrestful respites from the outside world. While I enjoyed the company of friends at dinners, I didn't feel comfortable sleeping in my old bedroom, for example. I needed to be alone and able to sleep when I wanted. Or watch TV late. Or read a book. Or just be by myself. When morning came, it was always a quick shower and off to The Angeles Clinic. I couldn't eat before my PET/CT scan, so I preferred to get out and go without seeing or talking to anyone. After blood work was drawn I would walk across the street to a diner or restaurant to get breakfast. My staying in hotels wasn't a snub to my family but I knew it felt like that to them. Rather, it was what I needed for my sanity.

The next morning, I awoke early and made my way to The Angeles Clinic. True to Cathy's word, the day took much longer than projected by Dr. O'Day and I didn't even start the infusion until about 1:00 p.m. During the infusion period Dr. O'Day sat with me for a while to explain in greater detail the potential side effects. Mind you I had already read a 30+ page patient consent form that explained everything in excruciating detail, but it was nicer to hear the highlights from him directly. I could expect flu-like symptoms, rash, itching, nausea and diarrhea. However, if I did experience all those symptoms, it would be a good thing because the side effects were positively correlated with a response to the treatment. In other words, if I experienced the side effects I was likely benefiting from the Ipilimumab. But, and here was the big but, if I did start getting diarrhea, I needed to keep track of how frequently and how severe were the bowel movements because if not treated promptly, the diarrhea could become colitis and lead to a punctured bowel and even death. I certainly did not want that, so I promised that if I did develop diarrhea, I would check in with Cathy at least twice a day. During the observation period I was fine, so I was released to drive home about 3:30 p.m.

For any readers who don't know Los Angeles traffic patterns, leaving the West Side at 3:30 p.m. to drive south on the 405 Freeway is like asking to sit in a parking lot for four hours. I was stuck in traffic past the Los Angeles Airport, past the beach cities, past the Harbor Freeway, past Long Beach, and all the way through Orange County. Finally, I got a little break for the last 30 miles or so to San Diego. But I didn't really have a choice. I was not inclined to wait through dinner to drive home at 7:00 p.m. after rush hour traffic finally subsided. So off I went and didn't get home until 7:30.

When I got home I was pretty tired from the long day and just wanted to eat dinner and jump in the shower. I started to ache a little but wasn't tired enough to fall asleep, so I just crawled into bed, pulled up the blankets, and watched TV. I felt fine the next morning and went to the gym per my normal routine.

That didn't seem too bad. Until about three days later, that is. That's when the diarrhea started. And within hours I was on the phone with Cathy detailing the severity. That was smart because she called in a prescription for a steroid that would help. The steroids didn't help immediately but the diarrhea began to ease after a few days. I also started to itch quite a bit, and in very uncomfortable places. But those were good signs, so I didn't complain.

During my second week after the first treatment my friends Chris and Scott came to visit. We had to cancel the April Chicago trip, so I asked them instead to come visit me in San Diego while I could still enjoy their company. With eight tumors, some near my heart, I wasn't so sure I was going to survive. They came for two nights and three days, and the plan was to play golf twice, go to a San Diego Padres baseball game and watch horse racing at the Del Mar Racetrack. The weather was perfect, and it looked like we were in for a great time.

I picked them up at the airport and drove them to their hotel to get settled. I then brought them home to see the family (they knew everyone as we had visited both of them before) and had a nice dinner. I picked them up early the next morning for a day at Torrey Pines. My brother-in-law John played with us in our foursome. The Torrey Pines South golf course is one of the most scenic and challenging public courses in America and runs along bluffs overlooking the Pacific Ocean. Neither Chris nor Scott had played there before. The first hole went directly west towards the Pacific Ocean. The second turned left and ran parallel to the fourth, while the third offered a majestic view, a short par three over a canyon with the cliffs directly behind the green. The fourth turned north adjacent to the cliffs and was so long and hard that it was not fair to the average golfer, and we were decidedly average. The fifth came back south and then we reached the sixth, a short par five that bordered a different canyon. And then it hit me. Nausea. And there I was puking my guts out over the railing while Chris, Scott and John were trying to tee off.

I made it through the next few difficult holes and we arrived at the eighth green. And this was when I started feeling the gurgling on the other end. Putting in golf requires one to be quite still. Putting is a challenge for a professional, let alone the average golfer. But it was even more challenging when squeezing my buttocks to prevent diarrhea. Next up was the ninth tee. Now if I described putting as difficult, the regular golf swing was even more difficult to accomplish while squeezing my buttocks. Lucky enough there was a snack bar between the ninth and tenth holes with a restroom. I took the golf cart and let them play the rest of the hole while I went to relieve myself. I can't explain how embarrassing it felt to vomit and have diarrhea on the golf course. But my friends were the truest friends in the world and they just wanted to make sure I was okay. They made the pain of embarrassment disappear. I love Chris and Scott more than I can ever show them.

We finished the round of golf then headed back to the hotel to hang out for a while. I let them shower and change while I went home to do the same. I picked up my son Sam who was joining us at the baseball game. We then got Chris and Scott and headed down to the ballpark. Being at a baseball game, of course we ate hot dogs. Somehow, I managed to eat a hot dog and not vomit. It was a fun evening and on the drive home Sam asked Scott if he'd ever had an In-n-Out hamburger. When Scott replied he hadn't, Sam, Chris and I responded simultaneously that we had to stop on the way home. To recap, during the course of the day we'd eaten a sandwich on the golf course, hot dogs at the baseball game and drunk many beers. Yet we were now going for a hamburger. For Scott, a Double-Double to be precise. This was a true gastronomic experience. I was so thankful that Sam got to enjoy this time with us. He gained an appreciation for the depth of my friendship with Chris and Scott.

The next day we were supposed to play another round of golf but mercifully Scott and Chris suggested we not play to prevent the same diarrhea/vomit routine. Instead, we went to a favorite lunch joint and then to the Del Mar Racetrack, where the turf famously meets the surf. Much to Scott's and my surprise, Chris had a convoluted betting technique that more mirrored an investment hedge strategy. We are both pretty smart dudes, and Scott was a Wall Street trader, but even we couldn't figure out what Chris was doing. But he won a few hundred dollars and that was fun. We had dinner with the family again and then I spent the night in the hotel lounge just talking with them before they left the next day. I knew that I was so lucky to have friends like that who came because I asked. The moral of the story was to ask your friends to come see you if you wanted to see them before you thought you might die. In my case, I didn't die, but I sure was grateful at the time for their love and support.

It was about 14 days post-infusion when I woke up to the oddest feeling. Overnight, my left jaw had blown up to about the size of a grapefruit. Seriously. It was huge and jutting off my face. I knew intuitively that this couldn't be a tumor because cancer cells needed time to replicate and multiply and they couldn't do that overnight. I sent a picture to Dr. O'Day via email and he responded as I had hoped. He told me that this was one of the fastest, largest reactions to the Ipilimumab that he had ever seen in any patient at any dosage level. I liked hearing that from him and wasn't worried – just uncomfortable.

What was crazy is what happened later that day when I took Sam to the orthodontist. In the prologue I said people may surprise you with their reactions. Well, the receptionist sure did that to me. She looked at me and with all seriousness asked me if I was aware that I had a large growth on my jaw. She asked me if I wanted the doctor to take a look. I couldn't believe my ears. Could she possibly think that I wasn't aware of a grapefruit-sized protrusion on my jaw? Could she possibly think that it wasn't so uncomfortable that I wouldn't notice? I found this exchange absolutely hysterical and absurd. As politely as possible, I told her that I knew about it and it was a reaction to a medication and I had informed my doctor. Thinking about this episode later always made me laugh.

At this point the steroids had kicked into full gear and the diarrhea had stopped. Finally. And within three days the swelling on my jaw began to subside. I was feeling pretty good. More remarkably, though, I could feel the tumor on my chest shrinking. As this was the most prominent tumor I'd ever had (the ones on my back were much smaller and this one was about the size of a peanut M&M candy), it was the most amazing feeling to see and feel a tumor shrink! Could the Ipilimumab be working, I thought? I'd gotten the other side effects (and still had the itching) and that seemed to be a good sign. I couldn't believe the feeling of making progress and resurrecting my hope. It seemed truly miraculous.

LESSONS LEARNED

> - ***Don't hesitate to share every detail about side effects with your doctor and nurses, no matter how embarrassing – it could save your life***
> - ***If possible, get treated at a clinic/university hospital where the doctors have significant experience with your treatment protocol***

The most important thing to remember is that when your doctor or oncologist gives you instructions about side effects and how to follow up, just do it. I know that diarrhea is very uncomfortable and describing the frequency and severity can seem embarrassing. But believe me when I tell you that your nurses have heard and seen everything. There is nothing you can share that will shock or surprise them. Moreover, the instructions are there for a reason – to keep you alive. Period. End of story. Follow their instructions to the letter – it can save your life. Don't hold back on anything that concerns you. And please use the nurse as your front-line contact. They are there to listen to you and advise you. If there is an urgent concern, they will find your doctor (or another one in the same practice) and follow up with you as needed. They will reach your doctor before you will and will likely know what to do without having to ask your doctor.

Another lesson for me was how important it was to be at a clinic that had a vast amount of experience with clinical trials, especially the one in which I was participating. Dr. O'Day had worked with enough patients that he knew when to prescribe the steroids and to keep me on the Ipilimumab. Some doctors without his experience would stop the treatment immediately when faced with that side effect but he knew that the tide would turn and that the steroids would work. I can imagine a community oncologist in a small town who sees one melanoma patient a year treating with Ipilimumab wondering what to do when the diarrhea comes. Hopefully she would follow the directions and prescribe a steroid, but would she know enough to continue the trial for that patient? Would she be confident in her ability to keep going? Or would she express her concerns to the patient and move on to other options? I didn't have to worry about that.

CHAPTER TWENTY THREE

Ipilimumab Visits Number Two through Six (August – December 2006)

Shampoo instructions say lather, rinse, repeat. I kind of felt like that's what my life had become. I had three more visits to Los Angeles virtually identical to the first. The afternoon drive to Los Angeles to beat traffic, the hotel the night before, the long day at The Angeles Clinic, the three to four-hour drive home depending on what time I finished, dinner and then aches and chills. Then feeling normal the next morning.

My second appointment at week three in the trial (for whatever reason, the drug company called my first infusion week zero) was so exciting because I couldn't wait to share the news with my nurses Cathy and Secela that the tumor on my chest was shrinking. I remember our morning hug being that much stronger. By the way, if I haven't mentioned it, Cathy and Secela and the other nurses all got big hugs and kisses from me every time I saw them. The infusion room was becoming my second family that I never wanted to have. But they were also the best second family you could ever have. Dr. O'Day later

confirmed that the tumor was shrinking and shared his enthusi-
asm to my strong response to the Ipilimumab. I couldn't be
happier with the progress I seemed to be making.

With this second infusion, sitting in the recliner for hours
watching the nurses work their tails off with no breaks, I had
an epiphany. I was in the recliner right around lunch time. But
I was going to be stuck for the next two and a half hours and I
was hungry. I asked Cathy if there were any restaurants that
delivered. She said of course and pulled out a few menus. This
was my aha moment. I didn't just order for myself, I decided to
order lunch for all the nurses in the infusion room. And thus, I
started a new routine. I had no idea that providing lunch for the
nurses would have such an impact on them, but it did. They
were so appreciative, and it seemed as if no other patients had
ever thought to do that for them. To me, they were my lifeline.
Why wouldn't I feed them when I needed to feed myself as
well? From that day forward, whenever I was in the infusion
room during lunch time, I would order or bring food for the
nurses as well. Typically, we would order Chinese or pizza as
they were the best options within delivery range.

The other part of my routine was listening to a carefully cu-
rated playlist from my iPod. Given that I was going to be stuck
in traffic for a few hours on the drive home, I took advantage
of the infusion time to relax and take a nap. It's funny that I
called that time relaxing, when in fact most other patients'
stress levels were at their highest. I don't know how I got into
this Zen-like state so easily, but it worked for me. My playlists
consisted of some of my favorite mellow rock songs from the
seventies and eighties – a little Stevie Nicks, a little Rickie Lee
Jones, even a little David Bowie. Another playlist was all new

age music like George Winston. Whatever the choice, the music was familiar to me and soothing.

About ten days after my second visit, after the grapefruit-sized growth on my neck had totally shrunk, it blew up again overnight. I shared this news with Dr. O'Day and he was ecstatic because this meant that my tumors were reacting to the Ipilimumab. That news made me very excited as well, which was only reinforced by the fact that I now felt not just the tumor on my chest shrinking but the ones on my upper back as well. I was also starting to feel the other side effect which for me was itching, and again in very uncomfortable places (my groin area/scrotum, tops of my feet, between my fingers) where it was very obvious to anyone around me that I was scratching myself. I did not like this side effect, of course, but it was indeed tolerable knowing that the tumors were shrinking.

Visits three and four mirrored the experience in visits one and two, with one exception. I was now on a regular schedule in the infusion room and I started to recognize some of the other patients who, although not on the same drug protocol, were on similar schedules. What made these visits different is I started chatting with and befriend as many of these "regulars" as I could remember. I felt like we were all in this battle for our lives together and the more we could share and encourage one another the better. While I hated the fact that we were regulars, I enjoyed the familiarity. And I guess I was glad to see the same patients coming back because in my mind that meant that they were also either improving or not progressing with their disease. The Angeles Clinic treated patients with multiple forms of cancer, so I might be next to a breast cancer patient or a lung cancer patient as easily as I could be next to a melanoma patient. I often times asked the patients who were more open whether they wanted me to order lunch for them as well, but they always declined. After a while, though, some began asking me for restaurant recommendations.

Another facet to these visits that made my wife so uncomfortable and led her to stop coming was the wait time between blood work, seeing the doctor, and being called to the infusion room. It didn't seem to matter what time my actual appointment was because so many other factors came into play, whether it was waiting for the lab to complete blood work, or for Dr. O'Day to finish with earlier patients, or for the Ipilimumab to be delivered and prepared for my infusions. This is when I learned the value of being patient. That's funny, isn't it? A patient patient. There was no way to predict wait times and I knew inherently that I couldn't affect the outcomes. Everything was out of my control, so all I could do was make the best of this time – whether it was reading or listening to my music. My noise-canceling headphones became my sanctuary to facilitate my patience. Suzie couldn't tolerate these waits and her impatience made the wait worse on me. I felt better when she decided to stop coming with me altogether because I didn't have to worry about her anxiety.

Visit five was week 12 and was a little different because I didn't have an infusion scheduled. Rather, I started the day on the CT scan machine to check on my progress. I couldn't wait for the results as the tumors on my chest and back had totally disappeared. When I was finally called back to the examination room to see Dr. O'Day, it was the best news ever – all eight tumors had disappeared! I had what was technically called a complete response to the Ipilimumab. I just couldn't believe it after everything I'd been through the past year and a half. I couldn't wait to call Suzie with the news. But before I left Dr.

O'Day's office, I walked back to the infusion room to share the excitement with Cathy, Secela and the other nurses. What great hugs those were. But I was a little deflated to catch the reaction from some of the other patients in the room. There seemed to be a mix of gladness for my outcome and sadness that they weren't the ones getting the good news.

The next eight weeks were relatively uneventful as I had no treatments or appointments scheduled. I was able to push forward on the Miracle League and put relatively normal hours in at work, even though I had fewer responsibilities now that the company had been acquired. But around this time, I could feel another tumor beginning to grow on my chest, just about where the other one had been. When week 24 came around (visit six) and I was due back for my six-month check-up and scans, I was already on edge because I knew the cancer had returned.

When I arrived early and walked back to the infusion room to have Cathy insert the IV into my arm and draw blood, I told her about the tumor on my chest. She gave me a warm hug and said not to worry, that the doctors would have a new plan. She also told me that Dr. O'Day wasn't in the office, so I was going to be seen by Dr. Omid Hamid. I should point out that one of the benefits of a place like The Angeles Clinic is that there were several outstanding oncologists available. It wouldn't matter who my primary oncologist was because each of the others was familiar with my file and medical history. I had met Dr. Hamid before as well as another colleague, Dr. Peter Boasberg. Together with Dr. O'Day, they were the all-star trio who managed all melanoma patients.

I proceeded to the CT scan room, then drove a few blocks to a different facility where I would have my brain MRI (CT scans didn't work on the brain). While The Angeles Clinic had a CT scanner and bone scanner in the office, they didn't have an MRI machine. It usually took a few hours before the MRI file was emailed to The Angeles Clinic for the radiologist to review so I took my time with breakfast and drank extra coffee while reading the newspaper. That morning I ate at my favorite place near the office, the Literati Café. But this was no ordinary day and I was frightened about what would come next. When I got back to The Angeles Clinic, I had to wait at least another hour in the waiting room until I was called back to see Dr. Hamid. That one hour felt like four, every second like a minute. There was no way I could calm myself knowing that I had cancer yet again. Nothing prepared me for how to react during that time. I remember trying to avoid eye contact with those around me and trying desperately to get lost in my music. But nothing worked that day. Panic had truly set in.

When I finally saw Dr. Hamid, Sandy Binder, one of my favorite nurses who ran the entire office, was in the examination room with us. Sandy was my first nurse at the John Wayne Cancer Institute when I was on my first clinical trial for CancerVax. I tried to beat Dr. Hamid to the punch and told him that I knew the scans would show the tumor on my chest. And then he said those words I didn't want to hear: "that's not what I'm worried about." Whoa. I didn't expect that. He proceeded to explain that I now had a three-centimeter metastasis on the right occipital lobe, i.e., a brain tumor. It never even occurred to me that melanoma could spread to the brain, but it had.

I think I started crying on the spot, and thankfully Sandy was there to hug and comfort me. I didn't understand how I could go from clean scans three months prior to having a brain tumor in addition to the other tumor on my chest. The Ipilimumab had melted away eight tumors and yet I still had a recurrence? I was stunned, and this time wished that Suzie had been there. Thank goodness for Sandy. I don't think I could have survived that morning without her presence and support. Dr. Hamid proceeded to explain that the next step for me was to have Gamma Knife surgery to remove the brain tumor. He referred me to the USC Norris Cancer Center where I would meet with Dr. Michael Apuzzo, a noted neurosurgeon and one of the country's experts in Gamma Knife surgery. I would also need to see Dr. Essner again to remove the tumor on my chest.

What came next was equally devastating – I was no longer eligible to begin the quarterly maintenance infusion of Ipili-mumab. The silver lining, if you could call there one, was that Medarex (the drug company that developed Ipilimumab) had a second trial called MDX-25 in which I would roll-over from MDX-08 and have a "reinduction" according to the original schedule of one infusion every three weeks for four doses. Following 24 weeks, assuming I had a complete response again, I could receive the maintenance therapy.

While Dr. Hamid worked the phones to get me an appointment ASAP with Dr. Apuzzo, I had to make several calls of my own. The first was to my wife who was predictably devastated by the news. I explained the next steps as calmly as I could, and that Dr. Hamid was working on an appointment for the next day. I told her that if it was the next day, I would spend the night in Los Angeles and have a friend go with me to the appointment. This was not the type of conversation that goes well over the phone, but the conversation couldn't wait. I wished Suzie had been with me at that appointment to both be my advocate and to provide the comfort I so desperately needed. But alas she wasn't. My next call was to the hotel I had stayed at the night before to book another room. Once I had the hotel room booked, I walked over to the infusion room to see Cathy and Secela. I was virtually inconsolable over the news of a brain tumor and they gave me whatever support and love they could in between treating the other patients in the infusion room.

Sandy came to find me shortly thereafter to tell me that I had an appointment with Dr. Apuzzo at USC the following day and that I was free to leave the office. It was now mid-afternoon, and I went straight to the hotel to lie down. But first I called my friend Jamie and asked if he would accompany me to USC. Of course he said yes because that's what great friends do. I knew that Jamie would be extremely objective in listening and asking questions. I ordered room service, ate in bed, listened to my mellowest music and closed my eyes early.

The next day Jamie met me at USC. I think he might have been even more nervous than I and it really showed. While we were waiting to see Dr. Apuzzo I brought him up to speed on the details and my feelings, and his compassion was overwhelming. I never would have imagined when we graduated law school in 1987 that almost 20 years later he would be the friend I would choose to visit a Gamma Knife surgeon. But then again, who would ever think that way? Nonetheless, Jamie and I had a special bond. After all those boys' nights outs during the CancerVax trial and Jamie's visits to St. John's Hospital during biochemotherapy, there wasn't anything we couldn't share. I was so fortunate to have many friends like Jamie whose support never wavered.

We didn't meet Dr. Apuzzo though. We met Dr. Paul Pagnini, the radiation oncologist who worked with Dr. Apuzzo, who finally explained what Gamma Knife surgery is and what it isn't. Gamma Knife radiosurgery, also called stereotactic radiosurgery, was a very precise form of therapeutic radiology. Even though it was called surgery, a Gamma Knife procedure did not involve actual surgery, nor was the Gamma Knife really a knife at all. Gamma Knife used beams of highly-focused gamma rays to treat small to medium size lesions, usually in the brain. Many beams of gamma radiation joined to focus on the lesion under treatment, providing a very intense dose of radiation without a surgical incision or opening.

My Gamma Knife procedure would involve a treatment team approach. My team would include a radiation oncologist (Dr. Pagnini), a neurosurgeon (Dr. Apuzzo), a radiation therapist, and a registered nurse. In addition, a medical physicist and a dosimetrist would work together to calculate the precise number of exposures and beam placement necessary to obtain the radiation dose that Dr. Pagnini would prescribe.

Jamie and I asked lots of questions but I'm not sure I could remember any of them as this was all new to me. I think we left extremely confident that I was in the right hands and with enough knowledge to explain the procedure. I don't believe I ever adequately expressed my gratitude to Jamie for his being there with me that day. I could not have gotten through the appointment without him nor could I have been able to explain the details to my wife and children.

I certainly didn't expect visit six for Ipilimumab to turn into a two-day affair complete with a visit to USC to learn about how to treat a brain tumor. My drive home that day was nerve-racking and while I couldn't wait to get home to see my family, I dreaded explaining to them the treatment plan.

LESSONS LEARNED

> - *It is advisable to have an independent advocate with you at all key appointments*
> - *Get to know and love your nurses and fellow patients*

I learned how important it is to have an advocate with you at all times. Although I became comfortable driving to Los Angeles alone and spending all day without Suzie, I realized the day I was diagnosed with the brain tumor how foolish it was not to have her or another close friend or family member be with me for every doctor's appointment, no matter how routine. Because no matter how routine you might think the appointment, it might not turn out that way.

I learned that I had tremendous compassion for my nurses and the other patients in the infusion room. These people share your journey and are sometimes the best friends you'll have. If you are a cancer patient, you learn very quickly that those who have never been patients nor cared for others diagnosed with cancer, can never truly understand your experiences. Try as they might, they just don't get it like we do, and that can be very frustrating. It is imperative to make friends with other patients and nurses, so you have someone with whom you can freely share the most difficult of details.

CHAPTER TWENTY FOUR

Gamma Knife Surgery Plus Surgery Number Ten (January 2007)

The drive home alone that afternoon was excruciating. All I could think about the entire two-plus hours was how would I explain a brain tumor to a 12-year old and a nine-year old, let alone my wife. How would I explain that I had a brain tumor and another tumor on my chest just three months after having completely clean scans? How would they face the challenge of more treatment after over a year of non-stop treatments? It was hard enough for me to grasp, let alone the kids. I had multiple conversations in my head, imagining Sam and Jordan's responses, and trying to figure out how to respond on my own. My emotions were running wild as well. Just two weeks prior, the Miracle League of San Diego donated its share to the County of San Diego to enable construction of our field. The negative karma didn't feel right to me.

When I finally got home, I had the hardest conversation of my life. I had become accustomed to seeing the fear in Sam and Jordan's eyes every time I told them about a recurrence, which was a horrible thing to become accustomed to seeing. But the fear this time, when the words "brain tumor" came out of my mouth, was deeper. The shock was deeper. The questions about what next were deeper. I did my best to explain Gamma Knife surgery, the next surgery with Dr. Essner and the chance to start the Ipilimumab trial again. I did my best to reassure Sam and Jordan that I was going to be alive for Sam's bar mitzvah the next December and that the next goal after that was to be alive for Jordan's bat mitzvah two and a half years later. I kept my strong "I'll beat this" face on, the whole time feeling like my insides were rotting and I wouldn't make it. I'd never been so scared and needed to have a therapy session with my psychotherapist Ellie.

That night we did our best at keeping close and hugging each other, but Sam and Jordan weren't feeling it. They were so scared but couldn't quite articulate that feeling. They appeared strong and confident, but I could tell that they weren't. Like their mother, they tended to hold these emotions inside and not let me see how vulnerable they were feeling.

All things changed the next day between Suzie and me as she was struggling with coming to grips with my bad news. Her fear of losing me turned into bitter anger and manifested itself in a shouting match that was extraordinarily harsh. Suzie lashed out at me for "ruining her life." I didn't comprehend that feeling since I was the one who was undergoing all of these treatments, not her. I was the one driving to Los Angeles at least every three months to get IV infusions. I was the one being carved up and building scar tissue in my neck to the point I couldn't turn my head well. I was the one who couldn't put in full days at work. I was the one itching all the time. How was that ruining Suzie's life? She still lived in a great house in a great city near her family and was a stay-at-home mom with two amazing children. I didn't get where she was coming from, which may have had a more profound effect on our relationship than almost anything.

The day got progressively worse as the arguments then began to involve my family in Los Angeles. Why couldn't my parents take care of me, she asked? Why couldn't they take me to the surgery? Why didn't I just move to Los Angeles, she suggested, and recover in their home? I was flabbergasted at this conversation. My wife didn't even like my parents, and resented that they were there for me in the hospital during the biochemotherapy treatments. This was a Catch-22 situation where she resented my parents but at the same time wanted them involved. Given my emotional state at the time, I don't think I effectively advocated for my needs.

I knew that Suzie had anger towards my parents, but to tell me to leave the house because I had a brain tumor? That made no sense. In my greatest time of need, my wife turned her back on me. I knew in my heart that this anger was just her way of dealing with her fears, but it didn't make me feel any better. At the time, all I really felt was the anger, and none of the love.

It was near dinner time and as I recall Suzie had her parents take Sam and Jordan to dinner to keep them out of the house. I remember calling my friend Dave, because I needed someone to talk to. It was Friday night and he was at a mutual friend of ours for a traditional Shabbat dinner. Dave did not hesitate in telling me to come over and sent me the address. I wasn't as close with this friend, but he and his family welcomed me with open arms. In the Jewish religion, Shabbat is all about family and love and being together and I really needed to be there with them that night. I am so grateful for Dave's friendship, compassion and support. They were a true blessing for me that Friday.

It was a little awkward when I got home, and Sam and Jordan wanted to know where I had been. I kept the message simple, that I was at a Shabbat dinner with friends. I tried to never give them even a hint of the stress between me and their mother. Saturday was New Year's Eve and I don't remember us celebrating at all. Ultimately Suzie rallied to my side and on New Year's Day we watched football before driving to Los Angeles to spend the night in a hotel close to USC prior to Gamma Knife surgery the next day.

I didn't really know what to expect as this procedure was unlike anything I'd experienced before. As I understood it, the radiation therapy I had before was very different. Dr. Apuzzo met with us at the very beginning to more fully explain the procedure. Then we began. The first step was to sedate me so that the doctor could affix a head frame to my head. While I was asleep during this process which only took a few minutes, I was told that the frame would be attached to my head with four screws. I got to see the screws and they looked like large machine screws that came to a fine point at the end. The picture below shows the shape and placement of the frame, but the actual screws were much wider.

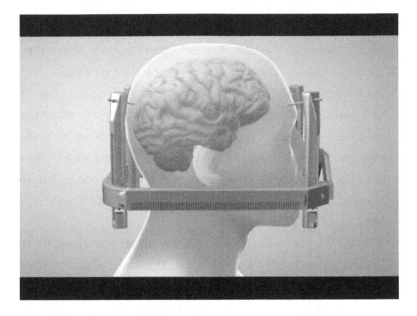

Once the head frame was attached, I was placed into an MRI machine to take a new MRI of my brain to identify the exact location, depth and size of the tumor. Many people have difficulty being in MRI machines as one can feel very constricted and the noise can be deafening. I never had any difficulty with MRIs and often fell asleep during the procedure. This time was no different as I still had remnants of the sedation in my system. Brain MRI's last is about an hour and a half.

The reason why I needed a new MRI, this time with the head gear on, was rather simple. My head needed to remain still and be in the exact position that it would be during the treatment so that the radiation beams actually hit the targeted tumor. Following the MRI, I waited for about two hours while the physicist and dosimetrist wrote the computer program to direct the radiation beams. I was still a little sedated, so I managed to sleep through most of this waiting time.

I was used to waiting but my wife wasn't and, moreover, detested waiting. The USC Norris Cancer Center was in a very isolated location a few miles from Downtown Los Angeles and there wasn't anywhere to walk. I know that Suzie brought books and magazines, but I sure wasn't keeping her company and since I was mostly dozing, she didn't need to keep me company. As a patient, it is hard to put ourselves in the shoes of our caregivers who wait countless hours without anyone to talk to or share, but I knew that this type of day was exceedingly difficult for my wife.

Once the physicist completed the computer program, I was wheeled to the radiation room where Dr. Apuzzo was waiting. He showed me this giant helmet that was going to be attached to the head frame. It had 201 holes through which the radiation beams would be directed. Once I saw the helmet I understood the reason that I had to have the MRI with the headset. Gamma Knife works by targeting all those beams through the holes in the helmet and if my head had been in a different position, or if the physicist had written the program based on my original MRI, the beams would not have hit the tumor.

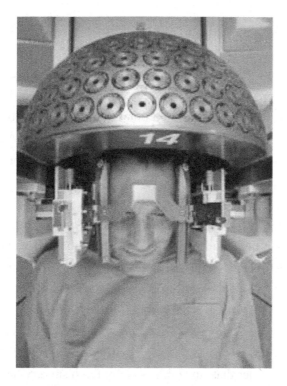

Once the helmet was affixed, the procedure itself took about 45 minutes. It didn't feel like anything and I don't remember it sounding like anything. Unlike an MRI or CT scanner, the radiation machine was not loud. Once complete, I was wheeled back to the examination room where my wife was waiting.

It had been a very long day at that point and I was anxious to leave. But first they needed to remove the head frame from my head. This time I wasn't sedated. I sat upright in the hospital bed while they began to unscrew the frame. It was very freaky to hear machine screws unscrewing from a metal frame affixed to my head. To this day, I can still hear that sound when I recall the procedure. This only took a few minutes and because the screws barely penetrated the skull (they really weren't screws but had a very sharp, pointy tip), all I needed was four tiny round Band-Aids to cover the holes.

We were free to go and off we went for the drive back to San Diego. My wife and I didn't talk much on the ride home. We knew that we had to turn around in three days to go back to Dr. Essner's office to remove the tumor on my chest. All in all, Gamma Knife surgery was a full-day, one-time only procedure that zapped my brain tumor with little or no pain, no side effects and no recovery necessary.

Having had nine previous surgeries in which I was required to spend a night in the hospital recovering, I decided that I wanted to avoid the hospital at all costs and asked Dr. Essner if he could remove the tumor on my chest in his office. Since it was just under the skin he said he could. On January 5th, three days after the Gamma Knife surgery, we drove to Los Angeles and went directly to Dr. Essner's office in his clinic. I joked with Dr. Essner that since this was my tenth surgery he needed to punch the last box on my card signifying that my next surgery would be free. He didn't laugh.

The next thing that happened was probably the funniest thing in all my time battling cancer and it demonstrated Suzie's very dry sense of humor. When Dr. Essner walked us back to the procedure room, he asked her if she was going to stay. With a straight face and without skipping a beat, she said, "I thought I'd video it to show the kids later." Like the stereotypical surgeon, Dr. Essner was very straight laced, formal and factual, i.e., he didn't have a sense of humor. His face about dropped to the floor and he just looked at Suzie and said, "No," she responded, "Just kidding Rick," and left the room. I thought this exchange was just brilliant and perfect under the circumstances.

Since Dr. Essner was doing the procedure in his office, I wasn't going to be sedated. Instead, he laid me on the table and injected lidocaine to numb the tumor area. It only took about ten minutes for the lidocaine to kick in and then Dr. Essner started. He placed a cloth over my face so I couldn't see, and he began to cut into my chest. I didn't feel anything and about ten minutes in, he had removed the tumor. Suddenly, I smelled something burning and asked Dr. Essner what that was. "That would be you," he responded.

He was cauterizing the wound to stop the bleeding. He stitched me up and the entire procedure lasted no more than 30 minutes. When I got up off the table, I asked him if the tumor had been sent to pathology yet and if not, could I see it. I thought it would be so interesting to see what my tumor looked like. It was still in the specimen jar and it was not at all what I thought. It was white, with blood lines running throughout, shaped like a peanut M&M candy.

We drove straight home from Dr. Essner's office and I was thrilled to be back in San Diego. By this point, I was so sick of being in Los Angeles because every time I was there over the past two years it was for medical treatment. Recovery from this surgery was very simple as all I had to do was keep the stitches clean. After about ten days, when the stitches were ready to come out, I asked Dr. Essner whether I really needed to drive back just to take the stitches out and he said no, Suzie could probably do it. Well, we were not communicating very well at this point and there was a great deal of tension between us, so I decided to do it myself. I found a tiny cuticle scissors and awkwardly reached across my chest to cut the stitches. That wasn't so bad. Then I began to slowly pull the stitches out and just like that, the stitches were gone. After enduring ten surgeries, I was now qualified to remove my own stitches.

LESSONS LEARNED

> • *Fear is a powerful emotion that can manifest in very unintended ways*

Fear is an incredibly powerful emotion, especially with respect to cancer and the fear of losing loved ones. Unfortunately, it is also a very difficult emotion to express. In my wife's case, fear was expressed through anger that unfortunately was directed at me. I'm not sure she meant to direct it at me, and I'm fairly certain her anger was at cancer, at the process, and the amount of time it took me away from family and work. It is hard when you are the recipient of that kind of anger to see through the anger and address the fears, especially when relations are already strained due to the constant medical attention. However, if you are ever faced with this kind of situation, honest and open communication is the only way to deal with the anger and to move forward with your relationships.

CHAPTER TWENTY FIVE

Ipilimumab Reinduction – MDX 25 (February 2007)

I was extremely fortunate that Medarex, the pharmaceutical company that developed Ipilimumab, had designed the trial I was on to allow a reinduction under a new study labeled MDX 25. Reinduction meant I would undergo the complete initial dosing schedule. That is, I was to receive an IV-infusion every three weeks for a total of four doses, followed by scans at weeks 12 and 24, and, if I showed no evidence of disease at week 24, I could start quarterly maintenance therapy.

Prior to starting, however, I needed to take a fresh set of CT scans and a brain MRI to establish a new baseline. I had an appointment scheduled for the first week in February and was excited to get the process rolling. But of course, as my history foretold, I had another strange hiccup in the process.

It was a Tuesday morning and I was scheduled to drive my friend Alton to an outpatient surgery center for a routine scope of his knee. My wife had left the house to drive the kids to school and I was sitting in the kitchen eating breakfast and reading the newspaper. All of a sudden, I became nauseous and got up to walk to the bathroom. On my way to the bathroom I became dizzy, couldn't make it all the way to the toilet and began throwing up all over the bathroom floor. I barely crawled into the room adjacent to the bathroom and curled up on the floor. I couldn't move and was paralyzed by dizziness. Amidst this agony, I was worried that I couldn't drive Alton to his appointment. Worse still, I couldn't move to get to a phone.

Suzie came home to find me in a panic on the floor and I told her what had happened. The first thing I had her do was call Dr. O'Day to ask if there was anything related to my cancer. He told her to drive me immediately to the Emergency Room and have them order a head CT scan. I was so scared I can't describe it. But since I made a commitment to Alton, I insisted that she drive him to his doctor's office first. While I lay on the floor I couldn't stop thinking about what had happened. Did I have another brain tumor? Was it something else? How could I get so dizzy and disoriented so suddenly? Thankfully she was back within a half hour. I was still curled up on the floor and totally disoriented when she returned.

I remember the drive to the ER because my head wouldn't stop spinning. I couldn't even sit up straight. The only thought going through my head was that I had another brain tumor and I was about to die. I knew Suzie was thinking the same thing and we did talk a little about that on the drive. She was so concerned and afraid as well, but I could barely concentrate enough to have a meaningful conversation. I managed not to throw up anymore and we arrived at the ER. I know the drive was only about 10 minutes (Suzie drove a bit over the speed limit), but it felt like an hour to me.

If you've ever been to the emergency room before, you know that the admitting nurse does a form of triage to determine how urgent your need is to prioritize the patients in the waiting area. Sometimes you're lucky and there is not a wait but this time there were many people there. However, my wife was able to explain my condition and medical history in a sufficient manner to get me admitted right away. However, it wasn't so easy or quick to have a CT scan. The first thing the doctor ordered was a sonogram of my neck area to see if there was any blockage related to my prior blood clot. When that test came back negative, I was sent to take a CT scan.

After the CT scan I was admitted to the hospital and moved to a single hospital room. I was being given anti-nausea drugs. When the CT scan came back negative, my wife and I were relieved beyond belief. Thank God I didn't have another brain tumor. But what was it? The doctor told us that I had vertigo, but that they couldn't trace the source. Hence, it was labeled "unexplained vertigo." This diagnosis permitted them to provide a different drug specifically to counteract vertigo. But I still had to stay in the hospital a while longer to make sure I could walk without getting dizzy.

What made this day worse for me was that not only was I supposed to take Alton to the hospital, but I was supposed to be playing golf in the afternoon with my friend Chris who had been in Las Vegas for a conference. He flew west to San Diego to be with me before flying east to his home in Connecticut. Chris certainly didn't fly to San Diego just to see me in the hospital but see me in the hospital he did. It was strangely comforting to have Chris there, and we reminisced about our last golf outing during the summer when I got sick all over Torrey Pines Golf Course. I loved Chris and the fact that he extended his trip to Las Vegas just to see me.

Early evening the doctor felt I was well enough to go home and released me with anti-vertigo medication, which included a patch for my neck. That was one crazy experience that thankfully lasted only a day. I was fine the next morning but still stayed around the house being lazy just to make sure. After all the cancer diagnoses I'd experienced, Vertigo seemed like a simple, non-threatening diagnosis.

Back to cancer-fighting reality I went and made the trip to Los Angeles for the new set of CT scans and brain MRI. These scans showed that I now had three lymphatic tumors in the chest and around my heart. The brain MRI also confirmed that the brain metastasis was killed by the Gamma Knife surgery and that the vertigo was just that. I was set to begin reinduction about a week later.

Back to Los Angeles I went for my usual night at a hotel, dinner with friends or family, then all day at The Angeles Clinic followed by my long drive home. When I got back to San Diego, I had a new passion to occupy my time. Construction of the Miracle League field and creating a league. I was officially unemployed as of January 1, 2007 so I had all the time in the world to dedicate to this effort. I had no idea how rewarding this would become.

In December, when the County Supervisors accepted the donation from the Miracle League of San Diego to satisfy the funds necessary to build the field, they authorized the Parks and Recreation Department staff to create a RFP process to select a construction contractor. That process was completed in January and a contractor was selected to begin work in February. Moreover, and this was critical to us, we had a date certain upon which construction would be complete and we could begin operating the Miracle League. Completion was expected May

18th, 2007 and our Opening Day was scheduled for the following day, May 19th, 2007.

The Parks and Recreation staff scheduled a ground-breaking ceremony for February 23rd and we rushed to find prospective players to be there. We were able to identify six prospective players and managed to order Miracle League of San Diego t-shirts to have them wear to the event. We invited the San Diego Padres to attend and much to our delight, the team's representatives included one of our favorite players and one of the Padres' all-time greats, Trevor Hoffman (newly inducted into the Hall of Fame). After the official ceremony, wherein our players had shovels in the dirt together with County representatives (this was a photo opportunity for them), Mr. Hoffman stayed and played catch with our kids. This was such an amazing show of support for us and beyond our expectations. Mr. Hoffman even took a picture with our daughter Jordan. This was especially thrilling for my wife who grew up a huge San Diego Padres fan and one of Mr. Hoffman's biggest fans.

Next came the hard work. We really had no clue how to find the players or buddies or coaches to play in the Miracle League and the instruction binder from the national Miracle League office didn't provide much guidance. What happened next was the direct result of my being treated at the JWCI. Ever since my treatment began, I became a regular donor to the institute's research, specifically allocating my funds to Dr. Essner, my surgical oncologist. I was even asked to join the JWCI Advisory Board where I met and became friendly with a woman named Donna. Her daughter was married to the son of John Lynch, a generous man who owned San Diego's top-rated sports radio station. Suzie and I knew that our best bet to introduce the Miracle League to San Diego and to recruit volunteers was to get on the morning talk show. Donna kindly arranged a meeting with Mr. Lynch and I remember how excited and nervous we were in his office. I was told specifically not to ask for anything, but rather to share what we were doing and let him offer to help. We gave Mr. Lynch our best pitch and at the end of the meeting, he offered to have us interviewed on the morning show and proceeded to walk us to the producer to arrange a date. That was incredible and the exact outcome we wanted.

The morning of our interview we were asked to be at the radio station by 7:45 a.m. to prepare for an 8:00 a.m. time slot. This was prime time and a great opportunity. We had written notes about what we wanted to say but were hesitant to just read them. We were walked into the studio during a commercial break and introduced to the hosts about three minutes before we went on air. The hosts, Billy Ray Smith and Scott Kaplan, were both former professional football players and Scott played pick-up basketball during lunch at the Jewish Community Center where I used to play. We'd played together before and I had told Suzie that he was a whiner on the court. As we walked in the door, the first words out of her mouth were: "Hey Scott, Dan played basketball with you at the JCC and says you're a whiner." Well, Billy Ray couldn't stop laughing because he knew that was true, and Scott became extremely defensive. Great, I thought. Now what would happen when we got on the air.

Lo and behold, we put on our headsets, the commercial break was over, Scott began to read our press release about the Miracle League and sign-ups, and then immediately started defending himself and accusing me of not being fair. In effect, he whined on air that he wasn't a whiner. Billy Ray loved this kind of dialogue as it was very funny to him. Scott took to using my wife as the offensive weapon against me and talking about her as the brains and muscle behind the Miracle League and I was fine with that. As long as we finally got to talking Miracle League, I was okay. At the next commercial break, after about 12 minutes, we had developed such a good rapport that Scott and Billy Ray asked us to stay for another segment to talk more about the Miracle League. We were thrilled and made sure to mention on-air that we were looking for volunteers and gave out the Miracle League phone number (my cell phone) for listeners to call. Scott and Billy Ray became great supporters of the Miracle League that day and have passionately helped promote our message many times over the years and we were grateful for that support.

As we left the station we were giddy with delight. The morning couldn't have gone any better and we had received a lot of air time to promote the Miracle League. We were barely in the car when my phone rang with the first volunteer. We had four more volunteers lined up in the next few hours. What a huge, unexpected success that turned out to be. We also recruited some family members and friends to volunteer and had our first volunteer meeting a week later. At that meeting, we came up with a strategy to deliver fliers to the primary schools in our closest geographic region that had significant populations of special needs children. One of our volunteers, Gayle, offered to hand deliver the fliers to every school. I'll never forget this because I learned the power of FedEx Office. I provided Gayle with hundreds of fliers and a list of schools. About two days later, she called to say she needed more but she lived over a half-hour from us and wanted to get the fliers quicker. I found out that through FedEx Office I could order on-line and have the fliers printed at the location closest to Gayle. She was a godsend and became our biggest recruiter.

I became a vigilant recruiter as well. Whenever I saw children with special needs in our neighborhood, I introduced myself to their parents and told them about the league. When I would pick Jordan up after school, I would get there early and stand near the front with several of the parents. The parents of the special needs children picked up first and I struck up conversation after conversation until I convinced four to sign up and be on the same team. This group of four became the core of the Miracle League Padres, and to this day, eleven years later, two still play on the team.

I also made a point of checking on construction at the field at least every two days. I delighted in learning the finer points of the process, while simultaneously getting frustrated with typical construction management delays. I loved seeing the old field being plowed over into a smooth finish to accommodate the rubberized surface to be applied above. I loved seeing the fences go up. I loved seeing the concrete being poured. I loved seeing the field surface rolled out. I loved seeing the scoreboard and sound system getting installed. Each step brought us closer to Opening Day and the reality of running the Miracle League.

In between trying to organize the Miracle League, I had three more trips to Los Angeles for IV infusions of the Ipilimumab. These trips became a little less of a burden and a little more exciting because I had Miracle League progress to share. One of the regular patients was a woman from San Diego with a young child. We talked at length about the Miracle League and I encouraged her to have her son register as a volunteer buddy in the program. She didn't but they did attend opening day.

This time around I was fortunate to avoid the terrible diarrhea and the only material side effect I experienced was the itching, which could kick in at any time. Also, after each infusion and the long drive home, I felt flu-like systems for that night only and crawled into bed early. I was always back at the gym the next morning.

Despite Gayle's strong efforts at delivering fliers to every school we could identify the player registration was slower than we had hoped. About a month before the season was to start, we only had 50 players and even fewer buddies, which meant we would only be able to field about four teams who would constantly play each other. On the one hand we were disappointed, but on the other hand, we knew that we would have a spring season and we would do our best to make it the best experience possible. But we were also concerned about ordering uniforms enough in advance to be able to put team sponsor names on the back. We were fortunate again to have made friends with the owner of a local sporting goods store who supplied a lot of baseball and softball leagues with their equipment and uniforms. He assured us that he would make sure we had uniforms on time and at his cost. It's amazing what people will do for a good cause and the Miracle League tugged at a lot of heartstrings.

Meanwhile, week 12 was quickly approaching, which meant a new set of CT scans to track my progress (brain MRIs were only ordered every six months). Because the three tumors I had when I started reinduction were lymphatic, meaning they were in lymph nodes deep under my skin near internal organs, I couldn't feel whether they were shrinking as I could the subcutaneous tumors on my chest and back. I had no idea whether the Ipilimumab was working this time around. I was getting extremely anxious as the day for scans got closer.

Week 12 arrived, and I made my usual trip to Los Angeles. No IV infusion was scheduled, just the CT scans, blood work and a physical exam and consult with Dr. O'Day. I had already established that I would be the first person on the CT scan machine every time so that my scans would be read early enough by the radiologist to enable me to leave Los Angeles as early as possible. This arrangement was similar to my insistence that Dr. Essner only operate on me if I was his first surgery of the day. Anyway, I arrived by 7:30 a.m. to get my blood drawn and then get the CT scan. I went out for my usual breakfast as I knew it would be at least two hours before Dr. O'Day would see me. After breakfast, my wait in the lobby seemed like it took forever. Finally, I was walked back to the exam room where I waited for Dr. O'Day.

One of the things I learned early on was that I could usually tell results by the facial expression of my doctor. When he entered the room with a very distracted or distraught look on his face, I could expect bad news. That day was entirely different. Dr. O'Day entered with a huge smile on his face. He quickly told me that the scans were clean and showed no evidence of disease anywhere in my body. He almost seemed more thrilled than I was, although that was not possible. I almost jumped off the table I was so excited. He told me to relax during the next three months and that if my scans were clean again then, I could start the maintenance treatment. I gave Dr. O'Day a big thank you hug then promptly walked to the infusion room to give my nurses more giant thank you hugs.

I couldn't wait to call Suzie and tell her, Sam and Jordan the news. That was one very happy phone call with a huge sigh of relief on all of our parts. Although the drive home was long as usual, I felt much more calm and alive. This was amazing news after this journey. Moreover, this news came just two weeks before our Miracle League field was set to open.

The hugs and celebration at home that evening were indeed memorable. While there was always a chance the cancer would come back, something felt different this time, at least for me. Because the Ipilimumab worked once on eight tumors, and then again on three, I somehow interpreted this to mean that Ipilimumab was the right drug for me. I was extremely optimistic with the family, and I think Sam and Jordan felt this optimism. My wife, however, was always the pessimist and waiting for the proverbial other shoe to drop, so her relief and excitement was a little more tempered.

LESSONS LEARNED

> • *Volunteer work is a great way to relieve stress, keep your mind off treatments, and find fulfillment when unable to perform your job*

Volunteer work at a non-profit organization is one of the most rewarding ways to spend time while undergoing intensive medical treatments. Volunteering is also an important release from the worries about your health status. It becomes impossible to think about yourself and wallow in self-pity if you are giving of yourself to the service of others. I also believe that the natural high you get from helping others directly impacts your well-being, both spiritually and physically. All the time spent raising money, working on field construction, recruiting other volunteers, players and buddies, kept my mind off of the treatment and prospects for the cancer to return, while focusing my energies on something positive. I believe in my soul that finding a non-profit passion helps you in life, regardless of whether you are battling a chronic illness.

CHAPTER TWENTY SIX

The First Season of the Miracle League of San Diego (May – June 2007)

We were two weeks away from Opening Day and construction at the field was still ongoing. Although the field surface had been rolled out for weeks, the fences, backstop, sound system, dugout benches and bleachers weren't yet installed. There were multiple other items on the contractor's check list that hadn't been completed either. I was beginning to panic that the field wouldn't be open in time for Opening Day, and, as it was, we were only able to have a short initial season of four Saturdays.

Although construction worried me, registration seemed to be picking up and I had to figure out how to create the teams of players, buddies and coaches. As I had never worked with the special needs community before, I didn't have an intuitive sense of how to group players. In mainstream baseball little leagues, there are tryouts and then coaches meet to draft teams, with initial selections usually being the coaches' sons. In the Miracle League, it was very different. I had paper registration forms (this was before there were on-line registration systems for sports leagues) that had detailed information like the child's diagnosis and special needs. I decided to reach out to the founders of the only other Miracle League in California where we had visited the past year and received some good advice. I wanted their advice on forming teams and they were spot on. Once we understood how to create teams, we moved on to other tasks.

Because the initial funding available didn't provide for a storage/restroom building adjacent to our field, we needed to rent a temporary storage shed from which we could also operate a snack bar. But how to fill that shed? What kind of shelving did we need? What supplies did we need? What would we sell? Who would staff it while games were ongoing? Again, we had tremendous support from family and friends. My wife's aunts Midge and Debby stepped up to help. They ran a very successful restaurant in Massachusetts and volunteered to not only shop for the shed but to run the snack bar every Saturday for four hours.

Most snack bars at little league fields aren't meant to be very profitable. Rather, they exist to provide basic snacks to furnish the players and their families at a cost to essentially recover out-of-pocket expenses. We were fortunate to find another aid in this effort. I had reached out to the head of the local Coca Cola distributer and was able to arrange a meeting. He was very receptive to what we were doing, and because there was no other baseball league for children with special needs anywhere in Southern California, Coca Cola agreed to provide all of our beverages for free (Coca Cola also makes Dasani water). Coca Cola became an important recurring sponsor for the Miracle League of San Diego over the years.

Other items we needed were appropriate bats and balls. Regulation baseball bats and baseballs would be both too heavy and too hard for our special needs athletes. Luckily, we were introduced to Mark Rappaport, a very kind and generous local businessman who had invented the Big Jack and Ball through his company Marky Sparky Toys. Mark had seen another Miracle League in Detroit and offered to help them. The Big Jack bat is plastic with a head that is about the size of a one-liter soda bottle. The ball is regulation size but is soft and designed to "fly" off the bat. Not only did Mark donate enough bats and balls for at least a year, but he agreed to donate a bat and ball to every Miracle League player.

As Opening Day crept ever closer, I worked harder with our partner, the San Diego Padres, to make sure that Opening Day was a great experience for all. As our field was designated A Little Padres Park, the club was incentivized to help. I had developed a great working relationship with Sue Botos, Director of Community Relations, who over time became a great friend and true partner. Sue was willing to help wherever possible. For Opening Day, she offered to send the Padres' mascot, the Swinging Friar, as well as several members of the team's cheer squad, the "Pad Squad." Lastly, she arranged for Randy Jones, one of the Padres' all-time great pitchers (he won the National League Cy Young award in 1976), to be our emcee. Randy was a very accessible star who ran his own BBQ concession stand at the Padres' baseball stadium, and I had met him several times over the years. Things were starting to really come together.

Opening Day was only a week away and we started to see more progress at the field. At this point, I was visiting once or twice a day to make sure we would be ready. I had now sorted all of the registrants into eight teams and had paired every volunteer buddy with a player. We had more buddies than players but that was okay because we anticipated that some buddies would have to miss games. Uniforms had been ordered and picked up and were ready to give out to players and buddies.

We decided to follow the recommendation of the Visalia Miracle League and held a pizza party at the field the night before Opening Day. All that was required was finding a Pizza restaurant to donate the pizzas. That turned out to be easier than expected as my first call to a local chain was answered and Oggi's Pizza and Brewing Company committed to delivering pizzas for over 250 people. San Dieguito Park, in which the field is located, has several large picnic areas adjacent to the field. We arrived with all our volunteers about 3:00 p.m. to set up all the tables with Miracle League decorations, to lay out the team shirts and hats, buddy shirts and coach shirts, and the Big Jack Bats and Balls. The pizza was delivered around 4:30 p.m. and by 5:00 p.m., we were inundated with a full complement of players, buddies, coaches and family members. By this time, we had registered 80 players, 100 buddies and 24 coaches. Our daughter Jordan was one of the first buddies and my friend Alton was one of our first coaches.

We couldn't believe the smiles and joy shared by all the new faces that evening. We never comprehended the extent that families with children with special needs felt isolated from other families, so when they congregated together for the first time, the bonds were immediate. The coaches were introducing able-bodied buddies to their special needs player and explaining their specific needs. Many of the buddies had never interacted with children with disabilities before, so there was a very real adjustment period for them. But the excitement and love expressed by all was beyond all of our expectations. So many parents came up to us and thanked us for bringing this opportunity to them and their families. For most of the players, they had never had a chance to participate in a sports league before.

We left that evening exhausted and exhilarated. We had met such an amazing group of people who shared our commitment to create something special in San Diego. I don't think I slept much that evening as I couldn't stop thinking about Opening Day and what I wanted to say to the crowd. When we arrived the next morning to finish setting up (we couldn't do everything on Friday because the contractor just finished their clean-up in time for our party to begin), the volunteers were waiting with huge smiles. The San Diego Padres had also donated "bunting" to be placed all around the outfield fences, just like you would see at any major league ball park for their Opening Days. We set about hanging the bunting and then the families started to arrive and congregate on the field. I had parents telling me that their children were so excited to get their uniforms the night before that they slept in them and never took them off.

It was time for the ceremonies to begin and we couldn't be prouder. Here were over 200 people standing on Engel Family Field (our major donors insisted on honoring us with this name), upon which construction had only begun three months prior. In a little over two years, we had turned Suzie's idea into a reality. In less than three months and with no prior experience we had successfully brought together over 200 players, buddies, coaches and volunteers. Jake Froman, the first player to officially register, threw the ceremonial first pitch to the Swinging Friar.

We played four games immediately following the opening ceremonies. I remember a businessman and philanthropist to whom I was introduced six months prior, telling me "when you talked about the Miracle League last year I couldn't envision it. Today I see it. I'm sending you a $25,000 check tomorrow." That was an incredible affirmation of what we'd accomplished.

I was overwhelmed realizing that just two weeks before Opening Day I had received my best news about my cancer in over two years. From that point forward, the Miracle League and Engel Family Field became my spiritual home. When I look at the photo of me from Opening Day, I see a smile that I could never replicate, although I try every Saturday I'm at the field. In fact, my facial expressions usually became warmer whenever I talked about the Miracle League.

Opening Day of the Miracle League of San Diego, May 2007

Engel Family Field – emcee is Hall of Fame pitcher Randy Jones

Jake Froman throws the ceremonial first pitch

One more memorable thing happened at Opening Day. We had a next-door neighbor and close friend named Alan Moore who came to watch and support us. He walked away with a compelling feeling that he had to help on an ongoing basis. As it turned out, our guest announcer for the day could only commit to Opening Day. Alan, on the other hand, had announcing aspirations since his youth. That night, Alan and his wife Donnel came to our house to celebrate a successful Opening Day and he told us that he wanted to be our permanent announcer. How could we say no to that?

Over the course of the next three weeks, Alan perfected his craft. We had this idea to have every parent fill out a note card with information about their child, including likes and dislikes. These note cards provided the background information for the announcer and Alan took to mixing things up from the notes. His wife sat with him at the scorer's table for the entire four hours it took to play four games. As a couple, they took over one of the most important and visible volunteer slots. But Alan didn't just announce games. He prepared an opening monologue for each week and created a different theme, whether military, spring training, etc. He gave this monologue before each game to set the stage. He also brought with a book that listed the minor league baseball affiliates for every major league team. If he was announcing a batter on the Padres, he might say, "Jennie was just called up from the Lake Elsinore Storm today to beef up the Padres roster."

Alan developed a set of catch phrases that always brought laughter from the crowd. While he was ostensibly announcing so the players could hear their names called, he definitely played to the crowd as the parents and other fans had a more detailed knowledge of baseball. We soon gave Alan the nickname the "the voice of the Miracle League." He was an inspiration to all.

During the course of our four-week initial season, I got to know every player, buddy and coach in the league. This process started while I was preparing spreadsheets for each team. I needed to get to know the needs of each player, as well as the respective abilities of the buddies, to make sure I paired them as best as possible. For example, we had one player on the Angels who was deaf, and we had a buddy register who said she spoke sign language. Seeing them on the field together was pure magic as you could see them talking and smiling the entire time. Getting to know everyone made the Miracle League experience that much more special to me. Although Suzie and I weren't sure when we started the Miracle League that we wanted to operate it every Saturday, I found that there was no place else I wanted to be. It was one thing to write checks to a charity I supported, but the rewards of getting to know the families whose lives we changed was unbeatable. Our initial season could be summed up as building a unique community and family. I couldn't have asked for more. When the season ended, and we gave out the trophies, the singular emotion I felt was that I couldn't wait for the Fall season when we would be able to have eight weeks of play and hopefully add more players and teams.

LESSONS LEARNED

More than anything, the Miracle League of San Diego taught me that I had so much more to give to the world than just being a successful business person. In just four weeks of play, what I got in return was way more than I gave in helping to create and operate the Miracle League. The gratitude expressed by players, parents, buddies, coaches and volunteers alike was heartfelt and overwhelming. I could never adequately convey to these parents how blessed I felt by being around their children. I was and continue to be awestruck by the impact buddies have on their players. I loved watching the buddies learn about their capacity to give and gain confidence with each week. What I got out of the Miracle League was a new passion and a desire to continue to give back in even bigger ways. Giving your time in such way becomes infectious and merely reinforces your personal desire to contribute.

CHAPTER TWENTY SEVEN

Life Goes On (2007 through 2017)

I made my first visit back to Los Angeles for my scheduled quarterly maintenance treatment in July 2007 after our first season of the Miracle League. My new routine entailed staying the night before with a friend, having dinner with that friend or more, and then spending as little time as possible the following day in The Angeles Clinic. I spent my first night in Hermosa Beach with Judy Petraitis, our friend from Manhattan Beach days. I remember sharing with her all of the success of the Miracle League. I found it impossible not to talk about the Miracle League to pretty much anyone who would listen.

I got up early the next morning to make the 30-minute drive to The Angeles Clinic to make sure my blood work was completed by the on-site lab early in the morning and to be the first person on the CT scanner. The way I figured it, the sooner my labs were done and the sooner the radiologist read my scan, the sooner Dr. O'Day could see me, the sooner I could start the IV infusion, and the sooner I could leave. If I was able to leave before 3:00, I thought I might beat the traffic on the freeway.

Although I was never really nervous that the scans would find any tumors, I couldn't help but be nervous while waiting for the results. That nervousness amplified during the waiting time. I was extremely thankful that The Angeles Clinic had a CT machine and radiologist on-site as my wait time was only a few hours. For most patients across America, that would not be the case, and the wait could be days or more.

I'd received the Ipilimumab IV infusion nine times before, so I was quite comfortable with the routine and expectations. I had loaded a new set of music onto my iPod and made sure to bring my headphones. I found peace and quiet in the infusion room and was able to nap soundly but for the hourly intrusion by nurses to check my vital signs. And of course, I shared all the pictures from Miracle League Opening Day with Dr. O'Day, Cathy, Secela, the other nurses and some of the other patients. Everyone was blown away by the smiles and the obvious fun. Amazingly, I was able to leave that day by 2:00 p.m. and beat the traffic home.

I also began another routine after I received the scan results. Because all my friends and family were anxious about the results, I began a group email with the subject line "great news." The body of the email read simply "clean scans again." This short email would in time become very important for all of my friends and family. Although I wasn't able to capture the humor that my wife was able to capture in her longer blog-type emails during biochemotherapy, the news was really what others wanted to hear.

During the second half of 2007, we had the wonderful pleasure of planning Sam's bar mitzvah party and celebration. Two years prior it had been my goal to be alive for Sam's bar mitzvah, so the celebration was going to be very personal for our family. Moreover, my wife's father had been battling prostate cancer and had also recently received good news, making the personal celebration that much more special.

For a typical Jewish parent, and for me in particular, the most important part of the bar mitzvah is the ceremony itself in the synagogue. Depending on a child's ability to read Hebrew and depending on your particular affiliation (Orthodox, Conservative or Reform), your child's participation could vary widely from another's. We were members of a Conservative synagogue and Sam spent many months practicing his role, which included leading prayers, reading several passages from the Torah and giving a speech reflecting upon what he learned from his Torah portion. When the day came, Sam was well prepared and calm, unlike how I remembered feeling at my bar mitzvah. I wasn't surprised, given how much he practiced, but it was still a nerve-wracking experience.

Sitting in the synagogue and watching the day unfold was one of the proudest moments I'd ever had as a father. I grew up in an Orthodox Jewish household and could only remember the relief I felt when my bar mitzvah service came to an end. I'm fairly certain Sam felt the same sense of relief. He had performed admirably in front of all of his friends and our family.

And then came the party at night. What a celebration that turned out to be. I'll never forget the smiles on Sam's, Suzie's and Jordan's faces when they each were lifted up on a chair during the traditional Horah dance. I'll never forget the feeling of holding Sam's hands and dancing together during the same dance – his Horah lasted about ten minutes which is not uncommon. I'll never forget how proud everyone in the room was of what Sam had accomplished. And I'll never forget how much it meant to me to be alive to witness it all.

What I always found interesting during my journey was how often people would ask me how I was able to handle all my treatments so calmly. Didn't I get angry all the time? Didn't I ever feel like giving up? Didn't I ever want to just scream and crawl into a cave? Didn't I ever doubt myself? Truth be told, I never understood those questions. I never once thought I wanted to give up. All I ever thought about was wanting to be alive to be with Suzie and watch Sam and Jordan grow up. I was depressed sometimes and sought help, but I never could fathom how anyone would just give up and not want to fight their cancer. After Sam's bar mitzvah, I set a new goal of being alive for Jordan's bat mitzvah, which was two and a half years later. There was always something to live for, and for me, nothing to die for.

I made it to this next goal, and pretty much every one I've set since then. I continued with my quarterly Los Angeles routine and of course continued sending my email blasts "Great news – clean scans again." Only the list kept getting larger as I would add new friends and people I'd encountered along the way who cared about my well-being. It was extremely comforting for me to send out these blasts as I knew how many people awaited and relished hearing the news.

The true joy in my life, aside from observing Sam and Jordan grow up into beautiful teenagers, remained the Miracle League. Every Saturday that I spent at the field reminded me that my troubles were nothing compared to those of the families who had children with special needs. I would spend four to six hours at the field, depending on how many games we had that day. I also coached one of our teams and the relationships I built with those kids and their parents was truly special. Engel Family Field became a spiritual experience. I began to describe the Miracle League to others as follows:

You could have the worst week ever, but when you came to the Miracle League, everything was right in the world.

We continued to grow our participation season after season and observed miracles after miracles.

One of the first miracles happened at the end of our second season in the fall of 2007. That was the story of Kyle, which opened this book.

During our fourth year, we had another one of those miracles. Hannah, a player on the Cubs, had an older brother who was her buddy. On his 18th birthday, he found his way into the wrong crowd and tragically lost his life. The funeral was on a Saturday during the Miracle League season. As the family and friends gathered at their home, Hannah's mother asked her what she wanted to do. She said she wanted to go play Miracle League baseball. As she arrived at the field, she told our announcer Alan that her brother had died last week, and she was going to hit a home run in his honor. When she came to bat, Alan asked the crowd for a moment of silence. Hannah then raised her bat and pointed to center field in the style of Babe Ruth calling his shot. Sure enough, she hit the ball deep to center field and ran the bases without stopping. Again, I can't retell this story without crying.

The Miracle League wasn't just about the players though. There were countless parents of buddies who told me that being a buddy was the best thing to ever happen to their child. I came to realize that our mission was very simple: to ensure that every participant, whether a player, buddy, coach, parent or volunteer, walk away saying they had a great day. Our wonderful community of volunteers ensured that we met that mission every single Saturday we played during the spring and fall.

The point of these stories is that through Miracle League, I learned that I had a higher calling in life than being an investment banker or high-powered executive. I realized that I was meant to change the world. I started that journey by changing San Diego with the Miracle League.

I continued to receive quarterly maintenance treatments all the way through May 2014. I was so fortunate to have met and befriended many of the leading melanoma experts around the country through my journey. After that May appointment, I had a group email with five of these clinicians to discuss next steps. All shared their opinions. Then, in December 2014, at my next agreed upon semi-annual appointment, Dr. Peter Boasberg looked me in the eyes and said the words I never thought I'd here: "you're cured." What a treat it was for me to send out my last ever quarterly blast email that instead of saying "clean scans again" said "this is my last one."

The Miracle League of San Diego continues to thrive and is to this day my happy place (we affectionately call Engel Family Field the happiest place in San Diego). In May 2017 we celebrated our ten-year anniversary. I was thrilled to share this event with family, friends and the greater San Diego community. Kyle Wyborney, who had "graduated" to mainstream little league, even came back to play with his old team the Angels.

Players and buddies gathered on Engel Family Field

Kyle Wyborney, late 2007

Kyle Wyborney with Dan Engel, May 2017

I still spend every Saturday during our two seasons at the Miracle League of San Diego. I coach two teams now, including a second in what we call the "Independent Division," for those players who no longer want or need buddies, and are learning to play by professional rules. I continue to recruit friends to coach with me and share the love of our extraordinary family.

I believe that the Miracle League, together with scientific advances and extraordinary care, are what saved my life. I was able to thrive through cancer by focusing on a higher purpose. I believe you can too.

CHAPTER TWENTY EIGHT

Epilogue

I've encountered many marriages that didn't survive bouts with cancer. Unfortunately, mine didn't either. I don't blame cancer entirely, though. While the challenges and struggles my battle forced upon my family were great, they only served to illuminate and amplify our existing issues. I can't precisely say when it happened but at some point, my wife and I stopped trying to fix our relationship. We'd become mutually self-destructive and I think, speaking at least for myself, resolved that our marriage was no longer worth saving. We separated in 2012.

As it turns out, the Miracle League may have had some influence on my finding love in addition to helping save my life. While browsing profiles on the dating site Match.com in 2013, I became fixated on "I'mJustRobin" and her incredible smile that looked like it could light up a room. As I read her profile, I noticed that she worked with special needs children. That was all it took for me to take a chance and write her a long personal introduction that of course mentioned the Miracle League.

On our first date, Robin acknowledged that she didn't read my entire introduction – it was way too long – but responded because she had attended Miracle League games for some of the children whom she taught. We had a great time and began dating seriously pretty quickly. One moment early in our relationship proved the Miracle League connection. I took Robin to the birthday party for one of the players on the team I coach. When we arrived, Robin recognized some of her past students, who in turn recognized her. I'll never forget Connor's reaction to seeing her. He said, and I quote, "I miss you so much Miss Robin. I love you so much Miss Robin." What happened next was even more precious to me. When we went to say hello to Connor's mom and told her we were dating, she stood back, smiled, and said, "I'm so happy you met each other. You're perfect for each other. I wish I had thought to introduce you."

Later, Connor's mom encouraged us to start the independent division in the Miracle League. Robin and I coached the new Miracle League Tigers together, while Connor's mom and dad coached the Reds. The happiest place in San Diego became even happier with this new division supporting another segment of the special needs community.

One of Robin's great virtues is her belief in the power of family. She helped me heal some of my family relationships that suffered over the years and brought us back together. I am so grateful for that.

We married in September 2016 and plan to live happily ever after.

ABOUT THE AUTHOR

Dan lives in San Diego with his wife Robin and their dog Dexter. He spends many Saturdays coaching two teams at the Miracle League which he affectionately and proudly calls the happiest place in San Diego.

In January 2018, Dan launched www.PatientTrueTalk.com, to solve one of the pressing issues patients and their caregivers face in the cancer world - a means to connect to other patients, especially when considering and deliberating over treatment options. PatientTrueTalk.com is the only pure patient-to-patient registry where patients and/or their caregivers can search for others with their same diagnosis or who have followed treatment protocols being recommended to them.

Made in the USA
Coppell, TX
21 August 2020